The True Identity

The journey to your authentic self.

Izabela Chrobak-Tysver, PhD

THE TRUE IDENTITY

The journey to your authentic self

Copyright © 2020 Izabela Chrobak-Tysver & beYOUtiful by Izabela, LLC

All rights reserved.

ISBN: 978-1-7332445-1-0

Book Cover Designer: Kinga Ciepiel
Writing consultant and editor: Hillary Beth Koenig
Publishing Coach: Otakara Klettke

First Edition
Self-published by beYOUtiful by Izabela, LLC
https://mailchi.mp/48f7ac888b24/true_voice
www.authenticwellbeing.net

GIFTS FOR MY READERS

Dear Reader,
Dear Traveler into the depths of your Inner Voice,

I'd like to offer you beautiful gifts to help you integrate the messages and tools in this book.

The Grounding Meditation "You Belong" will help you to settle and get grounded before taking on any task or challenges. https://mailchi.mp/67db2506b271/youbelong

The Heart-Connecting Practice will help you connect with your Heart, the place where your Inner Voice lives.
https://mailchi.mp/38b92e82a19b/heart

The Morning Prayer to Rejoice in Your Day is a beautiful mantra-based invocation to start your day knowing that there is something bigger that supports and holds you.
https://mailchi.mp/9040a108718b/morning_prayer

The Anxiety-Calming Meditation is a powerful tool to soothe your anxious mind, bring the feeling of safety to your body and compassion toward yourself.
https://mailchi.mp/75fa222f2100/anxiety-calming

I hope you find these gifts empowering.
I hope the tools I am providing will guide you toward the beautiful Inner Voice you own!

Love ♡
Izabela

Scan this to
receive bonuses

Sat Nam.

DEDICATION

I dedicate this book
to the strongest women I have ever met
my Mom
and
my Little Girl

CONTENTS

AUTHENTIC WELLBEING

The company Authentic Wellbeing was created in 2014 under the name of MDSB, standing for Motivation, Dedication, Strength, and Beauty. In 2016, the MDSB rebranded into beYOUtiful, which sounded not only more original but resonated with the core mission of the company and the work we do.

Today the company serves under the name Authentic Wellbeing.

I get asked often why I eventually chose this name.

Authenticity, emotional and spiritual wellbeing, and inner beauty were the leading morals when creating my company. I have always believed that no matter how beautiful we are on the outside, or are perceived to be by the outer world, the true and real self-worth, confidence, beauty, and wellbeing resides inside of us. It is unshakable, unbreakable, and unlimited. It doesn't need to be approved, proven, and validated by others. It is truly there, during good and bad days.

Moreover, I truly believe that a person can be as real and true to themselves and the world as they are integral and beautiful at the same time within themselves. There is no sexier and more attractive thing in this world than being strong and vulnerable at the same time. There is nothing prettier than being beautiful in the heart and soul. There is nothing more empowering than being kind and compassionate with yourself.

The mission of Authentic Wellbeing is that of creating a safe, open, authentic, loving, and empowering environment for every single girl and woman to grow, flourish, and realize the power and beauty within them. The enormous treasure of energy, wisdom, and limitless love every single beautiful lady possesses is the most magical gift they could ever ask for. My life purpose, and so the purpose of Authentic Wellbeing, is that of helping you create the fabulous and worthy person that you are.

As a transformational and spiritual coach of Authentic Wellbeing, I help women of every age commit to finishing their struggle with any relationships in their lives: the romantic ones or the job-related, the ones in their families, and the most important one, the relationship with themselves, including their bodies and femininity.

I work with women who:

1. Don't believe in themselves.
2. Have lost their feelings of worthiness.
3. Feel that they are not enough.
4. Are feeling tired of pleasing others.
5. Worry about what others will say.
6. Are afraid of judgment and rejection.
7. Are feeling lost in their own lives.

8. Have no clue who they are.

9. Have no idea what they want to do.

10. Are struggling with self-worth and self-love.

11. Fear not being loved.

12. Have had enough of the situation they are in.

13. Can't imagine they may be successful.

14. Struggle with anxiety and depression.

15. Experience trauma in their lives.

16. Don't see the light at the end of the tunnel.

17. Dream big but are afraid to go for it.

18. Lack support and encouragement.

19. Want to change their lives at the physical, mental, and emotional levels.

20. Are looking for something deeper within.

21. Want to embody the feminine goddess within.

22. Want to tap into their menstrual cycle.

23. Want to align their lives with their inner cycle.

24. Want to embrace and deepen their spirituality.

25. Want to find and reconnect with themselves.

26. Want to be the woman they thrive to be!

Is this YOU?

When I started meeting women who reached out to me seeking freedom, lightness, and alignment within themselves, feeling totally lost, miserable, and stuck in their recent lives, I couldn't help but interact with them.

I couldn't help but hear their deep cries!

I wanted to find out what made a woman feel unworthy, not

enough, unattractive, lonely, miserable, and like she had no energy, drive, or motivation.

What makes you feel like you can't fulfill your dreams?
What makes you feel that others are better?
What makes you feel that you don't deserve happiness, love, and abundance?
What makes you feel hateful towards yourself?
Why don't you like your body, your actions, or yourself?
What can help you to see who you are?

Why don't you believe you can write a book, run a company, have a loving partner and family, be happy as a single woman, or have plenty of non-toxic friends?

I hear you telling me:

- "I hate myself; I can't look at myself in the mirror."
- "I hate my body and how I look."
- "I can't possibly do that."
- "I am not enough."
- "I couldn't do that before so what makes you think I can now?"
- "I am not smart enough."
- "I don't have resources to start up my business."
- "I always date bad guys."
- "I am not meant to have a family."
- "My parents told me I will never succeed."
- "I am not confident at all and never will be."
- "There is no way anybody can see me as attractive."
- "I dieted all my life; I hate my body for what it does

and how it makes me look."
- "I am so ashamed of myself."
- "I can't get naked in front of my partner."
- "How can I love myself?"
- "I have never known who I actually am."
- "I need to take care of others first. I have no time for myself."
- "I don't deserve that."
- "I was always told to not be seen and to never be heard."
- "I have no hope."
- "I have no voice."
- "I was told to take care of others because this is what women do."
- "Taking care of myself is selfish."
- "I am not connected to myself at all."
- "I don't know how to be fully feminine."
- "I don't know what being feminine and in alignment means."

I hear you!
I feel your pain!
I see your situation!
I imagine your struggle!

I am sad seeing the enormous beauty in every single one of you, yet you hate yourself.
I am sad seeing the strength in you, yet you feel totally weak.
I am sad seeing the opportunities for you, yet you don't believe in yourself.

I am sad seeing the attractiveness in you, yet you feel unworthy of love.

It is heartbreaking seeing others stuck in a life they are unhappy with, yet they don't even know how it happened.

I am sad because I know how being lost, self-hateful, heart-broken, abused and used, and not seeing the light at the end of the tunnel feels. It doesn't feel freeing at all. It doesn't feel empowering. It doesn't feel like there is anything in your life at all.

However, I know how much energy, power, true voice, drive, and inner wisdom you have.

I am happy because I know deep inside that you are done with being where you currently are in your life.
I am happy because I see the sparks inside of you that are just waiting to be ignited.
I am happy because I know you are ready now!
I am happy because I know there is a way out for you!

There is a way out!!
This is your deepest self talking to you now and telling you that you are worthy of happiness.

Are you ready?

You got this beYOUtiful! ♡

Authentic Wellbeing offers:

- Signature group programs – "I matter" - helping women find their femininity, self-worth, and confidence by connecting to their bodies on the most intimate level;

and "Just be" - helping women align with their true selves, practice self-love and create a peaceful and safe space for them to flourish.

- Powerful one-on-one coaching sessions.
- The magical and inspirational "beYOUtiful YouTube Show" - sharing loving messages and coaching episodes including tips and free tools you can implement into your daily life and achieve personal transformation.
- The blog "Unlimited You" where you can read articles ranging from topics like health, fitness, body image and body movement, to life and success stories, abundance and money, to psychology, spirituality, love, sex, and desires.
- Lots of freebies and resources on the platform and website.

All of these follow closely and strictly with the mission statement of the company, providing women with the tools to help them uncover the enormous potentials within themselves, so they can create the lives they are truly meant to live.

The future plans of Authentic Wellbeing are to organize women's retreats and workshops, participate in motivational speaking at women's events, and create a worldwide community of women standing tall and true to themselves.

The future project for Authentic Wellbeing is to create The Dream Foundation "I matter" for girls and young ladies, helping them discover and rediscover their true potential and fulfill their dreams. The foundation's goal is to gather specialists in the areas of psychology, counseling, holistic coaching and nutrition, body movement, cycle and fertility awareness, spirituality, personal development, art, creativity, yoga, meditation, and many more to help every single woman find their safe space, connect to their bodies and femininity, feel bonded and understood, and become their true selves. The foundation's dream is to help women accomplish their deepest dreams by providing support, mentoring, and guidance as they travel their path to fulfillment.

PROLOGUE

I see a little girl on the floor.
I see a little body on the floor.

She is wearing a dress which looks like one you may buy at a cheap Chinese Market–pink and white, with random flowers all over. Her hair is amazing; The curls all over her head are infinite, like little rings.

It is late afternoon. The curtains dim the light inside, so it feels like early evening. I can't see if she is moving. Maybe she is playing hide-and-seek with her sibling. The silence is deadly.

I wait.

There is no movement for a couple of minutes. She is very still.

I see her little body curled up in the fetal position on the floor behind the staircase. She is quiet. Is she sleeping?

Slowly, I take a step forward, making sure that the floor doesn't squeak. I start getting concerned so I make more confident moves. I don't worry about the noise anymore.

I see her little body shiver. She senses me coming. She curls up more, bringing her knees closer to her chest and chin. Her little hands and knuckles are white from squeezing her knees to keep them close to her body. She is so quiet that I can hardly hear her breathing, even though I am just one step away from her.

I have waited long enough. I am deeply worried. I call out, "Hey, are you all right?"

She raises her head very slowly, still trying to hide it in her little hands. At first, it looks like she was sleeping and she is not used to the light which hits her face with the late sunset stream. As her face lights up, I see her round cheeks, the red marks on her forehead and the huge, wide-open, blue eyes.

Her eyes radiate a huge pain. I look into them and get goosebumps. She is scared. She is so painfully afraid of something. She doesn't want to look into my eyes as she fears I might know exactly what is going on. Her gaze is shy. Her posture is tighter. Her body language communicates her desire to run away. She is afraid of either me or something beyond imagination.

I kneel. She sits tight, protecting herself from any further harm. As I kneel, I reach out my arm to her, comforting her by putting my hand on her shoulder. She doesn't move, but shivers. In a gentle, kind, and loving voice, I ask, "What is going on?"

As soon as she hears my voice, she jumps up into my arms. My voice reassures her that I am not a threat and that I am not here to hurt her. Does she actually recognize my voice? Does she think I am someone she may know? Does she actually trust me?

She appears to be strong for such a little person. Her little arms wrap around my waist, pressing against me, so we almost fall backward. I stand up, keeping her close to my body. She refuses to let me go. She remains quiet while I get up and make sure we both are safe.

She doesn't express any other feelings beyond the extreme and undefined fear I see in the depth of her blue eyes. I do not understand how these little eyes have room for the amount of horror they see.

As we stand up, she loosens up a little. This gives me a chance to detach her from my waist, kneel in front of her and look into her eyes for the first time. She is more comfortable with me, however, still shy. I am a stranger, so she has full right to be shy and afraid.

Something deep inside of me is telling me that we have known each other for a very long time. It is time for me to actually figure out what is going on here.

"Hey little girl, are you ok?" She nods her head.

"Why were you on that floor?" She gazes away from me.

"What are you afraid of?" She moves closer to me with an expression of begging on her face - one that says take me away from here.

"Is there anything in this house you want me to take care of?" I ask, thinking that maybe there is a spider upstairs in her room. Who knows, phobias, especially to a little girl like her, might be perceived as life-threatening. And it didn't seem that her parents or anybody else were home. She shook her head, saying, "No, no, no, no, no, no." I got it. There must be something else.

"Listen to me, it seems that your parents are not at home. I just want to tell you that you are safe," I say. She hugs me again.

I hear her quick breath of relief. Her body relaxes but she keeps holding onto me. It appears to me that she wants to stay with me. I decided to be there for her. Her parents will surely come home soon.

I tell her she is safe. She repeats "I am safe, I am safe, I am safe."

The vision ended. I was sitting on my meditation pillow with tears running down my face. I felt heavy and light at the same time. I was sure I knew her. I knew she knew who I was. I felt what she was going through and what she was afraid of. I knew why she trusted me. I knew she was waiting for me.

I felt a sense of disappointment in myself. I was angry. How could I possibly do that to her? Yes, it was me who made her scared, and who caused her pain. I didn't want to hurt anybody, yet I hurt this beautiful little soul. I started repeating over and over, "I am safe, you are safe, we are safe." Chanting gave me peace and allowed me to become calm.

I recognize the truth.

That little girl was *me, little Izabelka* (as my mom used to call me).

She was there, all curled up, scared, hurting, alone, and with nobody to trust – and I had abandoned her. She was waiting for me to come and pick her up so I could assure her that she was safe. That we were both safe.

The tears of relief poured down my face. I breathed heavily.

I am no longer mad at myself nor upset. I am relieved, happy, at peace, and calm. I know she is in my arms now; she is safe, and so am I. I know that I will never, ever again leave Little Izabelka behind.

She is going with me, on the journey I call *my life – our life –* to the destination I call *my soul's purpose and assignment.*

I named it *the journey to the true identity.*

INTRODUCTION

In today's world, there is nothing more complex and frustrating than the lack of honesty and trust among people, with this being the major reason for experiencing feelings of loneliness and worthlessness.

- *Do you feel lonely and worthless?*
- *Can you say that you truly trust other people?*
- *Is speaking your truth and being real to people causing you to be anxious and afraid of judgment?*
- *When was the last time you had a real and raw conversation with a person, without hiding who you are or being afraid of rejection?*

I am going to guide you through steps that will help you become a person of truth, honesty, and rawness while maintaining your identity. The solutions I am going to present to you will make you feel worthy and confident enough to speak your voice, without being afraid of judgment or rejection.

This book is for people who are frustrated with trying to please others and pretending to be who they are not.

The moment I reconnected with my Inner Child (sometimes

referred to in this book as the Inner Girl or Izabelka) was the moment I discovered who I really was and who I was *not*. All of my life I had searched for that gift, or assignment, or mission, or you can even call it a universal or divine purpose — or simply a life purpose.

Reconnecting truly with who I was innately born to be and who I have lost connection to during adulthood was a call to come back home, where I had always belonged. The feeling of belonging is what we all long for.

Like many of you, I felt lost in my life. I felt like there was no job that would make me feel successful or un-abused. Shouldn't working for 16 hours a day, hustling and pushing through, give me the success I had always dreamed about, and that sweet approval from family members and friends? Do you seek that, too?

There was no relationship I would be happy in. Each of them were worse and worse. Was I actually a bad person? "You don't know how to love" - I heard it many times! Does that sound familiar?

It felt like I would never be happy with my body, too. The never-ending bulimia and eating disorder occurrences were a big part of my entire life. I felt like I needed to learn how to be that messed up girl and stick to it, never saying a thing about it, because no one would love me anymore. The shocking conclusions that suicide was plan B when the depression hit scared many friends of mine. It also scared me. What is your relationship with your body?

"They don't walk in my shoes." – I constantly repeated to

myself when someone judged me, or accused me of working too much, being anti-social, or being overtired.

"You are a piece of shit," and "You will never accomplish and achieve anything in your life" was autoplaying in my ears every time I failed at something.

"Failures are for the weak. Failures just prove the point that you won't make it. Honesty and authenticity shouldn't see the daylight. Actually, they shouldn't see the night light, either."

"You are just a piece of meat to use and abuse. Open your legs, this is your worth."

Does that resonate deeply with you?

If you find yourself in any of the above situations and statements, then this book is for you.

It is clearly going to help you gain enough self-confidence and self-worth to speak up, be honest, and never be afraid of judgment, rejection, or not being loved.

The idea to write this book came to me four years ago. The day I decided to start writing I received signs from the Universe.

That day, I was supposed to put music on, relax, and dance. After that I made my morning Yogi tea which had the tag with a mantra, *"Not sharing is not caring."* It was a call to my heart and soul – a call to my life's purpose!

I knew I needed to get to work. The world couldn't wait anymore for this book.

In order to do that, I needed to become raw, vulnerable, authentic, and pure. It wasn't an easy decision and task. But I knew it was a decision I needed to make for myself.

This is who I truly was, even though I had managed to hide it from the world so far. And that became the intention to create this work.

I never knew how to lie. I never had a poker face during conversations. I could never sugarcoat my speeches or writings. I have always found honesty to be the only way. However, the fear of rejection and judgment played an unfair game with me, and I needed to give in for some time - like all of us do.

Did it feel all right? NO!

Did it work the way I wanted? Oh yes, I had plenty of attention and external validation which made me feel sexy, wanted, loved, and powerful. I had a massive amount of friends to party with. I was the most wanted and valued trainer at the gym, where I worked at that time.

However, there were many times I had to shut up instead of speaking up when others were treating me poorly.

When I opened my company called *Authentic Wellbeing,* all I could sense was judgment, gossip, and negative talk behind my back. Was I afraid? –Yes. Was I hesitant? – Yes. Did I doubt myself? – Yes.

However, the most significant fear I had at that time was not being able to be myself; true, real, and honest. I was afraid of not being able to coach with the total alignment of my core values and integrity level - which, by the way, were way higher than that of the people I was surrounded by.

It was time for me to take a life inventory of not only how I used to live and who I used to be, but who I was hanging out with, too.

One day, I expressed my fears to a friend of mine I could trust, and I knew he also had a "weird" way of looking at this world. Being "weird" is a compliment I greatly appreciate each time I receive it. I strongly resonated with the feeling of being from a different planet.

I will never forget the words my friend said that day, "Izabela, you need to be you. You need to be true to yourself and honest. You are authentic. And believe me, people will love you because the world craves honesty, authenticity, vulnerability, genuineness, and truth. People feel safe and they trust you when you are just yourself."

So today I ask you -

- *Do you want to be around trustworthy people?*
- *Do you want to become a person of true values who others will honor, respect, and love?*

I am going to show you how!

Within this book, and as my job as a transformational and spiritual coach, I am going to show you how to tap inside yourself - dig deeper inside of you - and discover who you truly are. It is time to peel off that mask you are wearing and become the true you.

Just be YOU.

We often forget who we truly are and instead, we believe we are small, limited, and powerless. From the time we were born, all we hear are shoulds, shouldn'ts, can'ts, do's, don'ts, and the other limiting beliefs. "You are unworthy," "you are not smart enough," "you are stupid," "you are a nobody," "you are ugly," "you are poor and will always be poor," "you don't deserve to be loved."

We are forced to deny our true selves so we can fit in, blend in, be loved, and be validated. Therefore, we put the mask on our faces and pretend we are somebody else, the cool person who is strong all the time, never showing weakness or tears, handling any circumstances, and being pleasing to everyone around us. But then we are people who can't express themselves.

My coaching clients never look back to who they were before entering the program. Their self-confidence and self-validation are enough to make them confident in front of any challenges in their lives. It gives them enormous energy and internal strength to conquer the world they have always dreamed about by living up to their real and authentic standards.

Today I invite you to change that reality of yours, which doesn't belong to you and doesn't create who you truly are!

By following the guide in this book, you will find freedom in being authentic, genuine, trustworthy, and honest. You will not only live the life you always wanted, but you will also be surrounded by trustworthy people who appreciate you.

It's time to stop being the person missing out on opportunities in life because you are afraid of speaking up, voicing your truth, asking for a raise at work, or expressing your needs to loved ones.

It's time to be the kind of person others look up to, admiring your genuine, kind, and authentic personality. Be the kind of person other people marvel at. Be the kind of person other people will see and say, "I wish I was that brave and optimistic."

Be the kind of person who takes action now.

Stop hiding.
Stop apologizing for your being.
Don't dress down to blend in.
Don't *shut up* when you know you need to *speak up*.
Stop saying what you think people want to hear.
Stop trying to please everyone.

The real rejection is when YOU reject yourself.

The tips and tools I am about to reveal have been proven to create real life transformation and changes. As you move from chapter to chapter, you will receive information that helps you gain insight into your true identity. By integrating these steps into your life, one by one, you will soon become the person you have always desired to be.

Take control of your life today and enjoy the new you!

Love who you are; love your true identity.

Be you.

Own your power and energy.

Own your lightness and darkness.

Own yourself.

Mantras
I choose myself.
I choose my true identity.

HOW TO USE THIS BOOK

I have read many self-help books. The ones which gave me the most intimacy and the space to open up and truly work on myself were the ones in the form of a journal.

I created this book to give you what others have given to me. I want this book to be true and real for you so you can give yourself love and time to embrace who you innately are. It is only with constant consciousness, journaling, reflecting, meditating, and integrating that we achieve the highest level of awareness.

Each time you grab this book, grab a pen, too. Sit in a place where you are not distracted. Give yourself 20 minutes each day to read a chapter and complete the tasks. Tap inside of yourself. Experience the thoughts coming in. Feel the emotions. Just simply be in that moment of reading and journaling. Return to it any time your heart is calling you to do so. Use it as a best friend with whom you share your most intimate secrets.

To make this book work, you must be fully and truly committed, with openness. However, do not judge yourself and do not over analyze the process and tasks. You must be kind to yourself as you would be to your best friend or a child when they are having a bad day, emotional crisis, or doing the work you are about to start.

Each chapter starts with a piece of poem from my personal writings, which you can read in the full collection entitled "Decoding Self."

Every chapter has an intention. I truly believe that the intention sets the tone for both of us, me guiding you on your journey, and you trusting me while walking on this path to your true identity.

I share with you throughout this book many personal stories. I don't wish to brag and impress you, but rather to show you how I relate to you and your struggles. I share these so you can see I am a human with ups and downs as well. Just like you. We are doing this together.

At the end of each chapter, I share with you mantras which you can use once you put the book aside. Mantras and affirmations are meant to be repeated throughout the day, during mediations, reflections, journaling, and free time. Moreover, they are more beneficial during hardships and moments of hesitation, to ground you and remind you why you are doing this. You can write them on post-it notes, placing them in places you will see them every day. They are meant to help remind you of your true identity at every step of this process and long after you have finished this book! The mantras collected here are part of the True Identity Affirmation Card Deck that accompany this book.

You are beautiful.

You got this beYOUtiful ♡

Mantras
I am beautiful.
I am doing this because I love myself.
I am proud of myself for making this change.

CHAPTER 1

I am grateful

I am grateful for
the passion I feel

I feel the inspiration
I get the drive
I feel the abundance of giving back to the world
   thank you

thank you

I am so grateful
thank you

In this chapter, I am going to help you see the beauty in every task you do. My deep desire for you is that "thank you" becomes the most important phrase in your daily language, bringing you light and appreciation. In this chapter, you will learn how to be appreciative of everything in your life, starting with your breath and moving on to the sights, smells, sounds, and the magic and the gift of life.

This chapter will show you that life truly is a magical, beautiful, and miraculous place to be.

My life passing by.

I was driving to work. It was 5:30 am and my body was already loaded with three cans of energy drinks. I also had a great breakfast - a king-sized Kit Kat candy bar. I am energized because I slept for two and a half hours. That's pretty good though. Yesterday I managed to finish the project as planned. It took me a little while; I left the institute at 1 a.m. - but I did it. It was rewarding knowing I was hitting my deadlines. I also managed to add a few more pages to my manuscript. When published, I would be recognized as an author of a scientific book - how cool is that?

Today was a new day. I was totally excited and the goal was to finish the next part of the project. The team of three people working for me would show up in an hour, so I had time to get all the paperwork done, and get equipment and materials ready, so they could hit the lab bench and start working without any disruptions.

I was the study director of this project. Everything was planned just perfectly. Every aspect of my life was on point. This project was given to me because of my high ability to multitask, work long hours, be perfectly organized, and have great leadership skills. The institute knew they could save some money with me on board as there would be no need to hire an extra crew. I managed to limit the need for a team of six to a team of just three people, because I could do the job of three other people easily. As the work moved forward, I had full control over everything.

Sometime between breakfast and lunch, when my people needed a break, I had literally a few minutes to walk down the hall and grab something to eat. I always made sure my team was well taken care of first. They had breaks so they could eat. They didn't work longer than nine hours - I wanted them to be rested during the weeks of the huge project, and I wanted my bosses to be happy, not paying too much overtime.

That day, as I was walking back from the cafeteria, I started feeling sweat on my spine. I started losing vision – things started getting blurry. My left arm became numb. Breathing became harder and harder. My friend, who was with me, asked me what was wrong. All I could say was that I didn't feel like eating my sandwich anymore and I wanted her to help me get to my office. Walking became harder. I wanted to speed up because the feeling of being weaker wasn't funny. I wanted to be in my office as fast as possible. Obviously, it was just a weak moment and soon I would be fine. I didn't want others to see me having problems. There must have been something in that sandwich. At that moment, a silly thought ran through my head "The KitKat is better for me than that healthy sandwich - I knew that."

I got to the office and the first thing I did was lay on the floor. I am a doctor. I felt I was just getting weak and my blood pressure had dropped. Instinctively, I asked my friend to bring the chair closer so I could elevate my legs. The blood would start flowing down to my brain and heart and I would get better in a minute.

Surprisingly, it just didn't happen as I wanted. I was getting weaker and weaker and the symptoms I was experiencing were making me worry even more. There was no other option but to call for an ambulance. To admit that I needed medical assistance was very hard for me. It meant that I was weak, that I just couldn't get up and keep working, and that I actually needed help. We are going to talk about asking for help and how important that is in order for us to become self-confident in chapter 6.

The hospital doctor gave me my diagnosis: *you have just had a silent heart attack*. "But doctor, I am young; I couldn't possibly have had a heart attack"; "Yes, you are young and you need to start taking care of yourself" - was the answer I heard.

My experience was life changing. I literally saw my life passing by in front of my eyes. I saw myself smiling. I saw my mom's loving eyes. I saw my friends enjoying time with me. I saw my siblings being all playful and stress-free.

I made the subconscious decision that moment that I needed to change my lifestyle as soon as possible.

In my coaching, I use the following analogy. The Universe taps you on your shoulder throughout your life when things are out of alignment. At the beginning, the tapping is light, little reminders of, "Hey you, something here is not the way it should be, please slow down or stop; do something about it." The tapping may turn into stronger shakes of your body, emphasizing that you haven't changed anything yet and it's time to do so. The Universe wants us to be well. She talks to us in different ways so we recognize that we are treating our bodies badly, maybe we are hateful towards ourselves, or complaining about our job and life. Whatever it is, the tapping or simple shake is a sign that something has to change soon. How many of us don't see those signs, or even worse, ignore them.

Those gentle reminders eventually turn into a slap so strong that many of us may never get up. I am talking about heart attacks, accidents, a death in the family, or the loss of a job or life partner. Those are messages saying, "I asked you, I was sending you small signs so you could make the necessary changes to either prevent some events or make them loving and life changing." Maybe you could visit your father, with whom you have been at war with for years, so you could forgive him and express your love to him before he passes away. Maybe you could ask yourself how you could engage more with a project or interact with coworkers in a kind way so you won't face the loss of your job. Maybe you could recognize how traffic makes you stressed and implement mindful practices to manage it so you don't end up in a car accident.

It is our choice to live healthier, to love more, to be present, and to decide to be kind and respectful. Every single day, you are given a chance to choose - do I want to go out there full of hate, complaining, and harming myself, or do I want to start the day in a positive, kind, loving, respectful, and grateful way?

My message from the Universe was: "Maybe you could change your eating habits so you don't end up having another heart attack." I was lucky; it wasn't the deadly slap. It was a strong reminder of how abusive to my body and health I was during those previous few years.

The lessons for you.

The experiences I described at the beginning of this chapter taught me important lessons, which I hope by sharing, will help you see beauty in your life, too. Take some time to write answers to the questions I ask. Use the empty space to make some notes and reflections, and if needed, use your own journal. Don't rush through all the questions at once. Read them, reflect, and come back to them if needed.

Let's dive deep into your life.

The idea of this task is that you take a silent moment of kindness to observe yourself. Do not judge, just observe, writing in your journal whatever comes to mind when you think about the following questions.

- *Have you experienced situations or moments when something was telling you to change the present circumstances?*
- *How have you reacted to those signs?*
- *How did the actions you took after receiving them change your day or life?*

If there is nothing coming to you now, that is totally fine. The signs will present themselves to you when the time is right. It is very important to give yourself the space and time you need. It is important that you are free from distractions, too.

This is your time a peaceful moment just for you.

You will recognize and find those moments when a Higher Power calls to awaken you and bring awareness to changes which have to be made. Don't force it, if you feel like you can't see it yet. Give it time.

- *Lesson one.*

I was beyond grateful for the fact that I was alive. You will learn in the next chapters that this event wasn't the only one where I was grateful for my life - the biggest gift we all have.

- *How grateful are you for your life?*
- *Have you actually thought of saying, "thank you" to the creation of life?*
- *What are you doing on a daily basis to celebrate that you are alive?*

- *Lesson two.*

I saw an amazing opportunity to change something in my life. The things I was doing simply weren't working. The beautiful thing about it was that I could make a decision to change that - and never, ever have another heart attack.

Opportunities to change something in your life are everywhere. Do you see them?

- *Where do you see yourself making a change?*
- *How would you feel once you have made that change?*
- *How committed are you to that change?*
- *Are you grateful for the opportunity to make a change?*
- *What will be the first step that starts the action towards that change?*

- *Lesson three.*

I learned that my body is a beautiful temple, where my emotions, feelings, thoughts, ideas, creations, safety, kindness, playfulness, peace, and love live. How could I possibly make sure that all of these are safe and taken care of? Are they nurtured within me? Or do I trash that container they all reside in called the body? Those were some of the questions going through my mind.

- *How do you appreciate your body?*
- *How do you take care of your body?*
- *Are your emotions, feelings, thoughts, and ideas important to you?*
- *How could you nurture the temple of your body now?*
- *How could you nurture the vessel of your heart now?*

- *Lesson four.*

I started to see small things around me and be grateful for them. That is the most life changing skill I have ever developed and worked on. Seeing art on a water bottle, or the candle light gently move, smelling the pages of the new book, and tasting the soft cinnamon in the tea – how beautiful life started to become!

- *What are the smallest things you can see around you right now?*
- *How do they make you feel?*
- *How could you appreciate every tiny thing around you every day?*

Use all your senses:

- *What do you smell?*

- *What do you hear?*

- *What do you see?*

- *What do you taste?*

- *What do you feel?*

- *Lesson five.*

I learned to say "thank you" everywhere and anywhere. I learned to say "thank you" for the help, for the compliment, and for the answer "no". I learned to say "thank you" to a stranger, to a friend, and to a cashier. I learned to say "thank you" when I am happy and when I am upset. I strongly encourage you to do the same. Start today!

- *Where and when could you start saying "thank you" from now on?*
- *Where could you say "thank you" now?*
- *When could you say "thank you"?*
- *To whom could you say "thank you" now?*

Appreciation and gratitude.

Appreciation and gratitude play very important roles in the lives of so many people. The more I read about powerful and successful women, the more I see that their daily gratitude habit is what made them the leaders and aligned human beings they are today. One of my role models, Oprah Winfrey, said: "For years I've been advocating the power and pleasure of being grateful. I kept a gratitude journal for a full decade without fail - and urge you all to do the same." Her encouragement to keep the gratitude journal and create the habit of writing down five things that you are grateful for every day is the most important and life changing lesson you'll learn from her and from me!

The moment I included this habit in my daily routine, and made it non-negotiable, was a magical moment of realization of how beautiful life can be. Every single day is our choice to make it amazing or to make it miserable. No matter what it is, you have a choice to go about your day with your head up and a smile on your face, grateful for everything, or go there and whine, complain, and blame the entire world for the choice you just made.

So today, just as Oprah encouraged me, I encourage you to go to the nearest store and grab a notebook. It can be small, big, pink, sparkly, black - whatever catches your attention and brings a smile to your face when you see it. Grab it and *start every single day with three to five things that you are happy and grateful for.*

This tool is the most powerful tool anybody can give you.

Combine it with the Heart-Connecting Meditation (download here: https://mailchi.mp/38b92e82a19b/heart) to reap the effects of gratitude rooted in your heart.

Take your life's fate in your own hands! Be in control of it; be the creator of it!

In the next chapter, I am going to teach you how to believe in yourself. This process is strongly based on being appreciative of who you are, what you have, and realizing how gifted you are as you travel your path to greatness and your true identity. Seeing what you have in your hands makes you believe in what you are about to do. It helps you believe that you can be your authentic self and be confident.

Mantras
I appreciate my life.
I am grateful for my body.
I am nurturing my body.
I am appreciative of all my emotions and feelings.
I am beautiful just the way I am.

NOTES

NOTES

CHAPTER 2

I believe in myself

beauty
never taken away from us
innate
natural
with us from birth

why does it have a tag
be this
be that

you are beautiful
because you always were

I want to teach you to believe in yourself. I want you to feel empowered, believing in your gifts and dreams. My deep desire is that you stop losing time and energy by self-doubting and hesitating, and see the potentials within you. In this chapter, I am going to help you recognize what talents and tools you have in your possession that can give you enough evidence to see the value in yourself.

I am going to show you how self-belief changes your

perception of life, blocking any obstacles standing in the way of your dreams.

I believe I am meant to help others.

I was very successful at my corporate job. I started at the age of 22 and continued to climb the ladder until the age of 34. I obtained my master's and doctorate titles very quickly. I become a very successful publisher of scientific reports, manuscripts, and books. I presented my data at multiple international conferences. I had a job with full benefits, an amazing salary, and lots of paid vacation days. It was a dream career and job!

I have always had a love of nature, plants, and biology. As a young girl, I had dreamed about travelling across the globe, filming documentaries about wildlife. I had dreamed about going to college and getting a diploma in biology. During the years of my education, however, I ended up specializing in molecular biology and genetics. That became my passion. I dreamed of helping people with AIDS and HIV, creating the vaccine to give them the gift of life. I had known from the beginning, when I was that little girl, that serving was my gift. So, I made it to the area where I could help the most, in medicine, science, and research. I became a researcher. The journey had its ups and downs. But I loved it. I kept my dreams high and fresh every single day, especially in those hard moments.

However, the higher I climbed the corporate ladder, the less passionate I became. There were moments of deep hesitations about whether this really was what I wanted to do. Was I really helping people in this job?

Suddenly, there came a moment when I needed to face very severe ethical issues and misuse. My integrity, core values, work ethic, and most importantly, the deep desire to help others, were severely hurt. Quitting my job was daunting, but it needed to be done. My inner voice clearly stated what was true to me. My health was severely compromised. The heart attack caused by the stress and bad eating habits was the final straw. I knew I would face serious financial problems once the income was depleted. But *I believed I was meant for more. I was meant to help others.*

The following weekend I launched my website for my own coaching company. I applied for a job as a personal trainer at the biggest gym in town and I got it. Within a week I was working in a totally different profession. I felt fulfilled and empowered.

However, I couldn't believe it when I got my first monthly paycheck of $246.90. I was shocked! How was I going to live? That was the moment I decided that no matter what I was going to make it! *I believed in myself.*

It took me around eight months to get to the point where my schedule was fully filled and I was receiving clients who specifically asked me to train them. It took around six months to get my first paid coaching client at my company. The feeling of accomplishment was beautiful. And the feeling of doing something right was even more magical. I kept reminding myself that *I was meant to do something important in my life.*

Helping others, and seeing their successes and life changes made me smile every single day. Coming to work, where even though there was still the corporate to deal with, was a pleasure because I could see the magic happening in others' lives. I could see that I was able to touch others' hearts.

I saw tears in my clients' eyes when they could walk up the stairs after having no hope previously of ever being able to do so again in their lives. I saw smiles on their faces when I showed up at their family gatherings. I saw love in my Down Syndrome client's eyes who personally asked me to sit at her side at the table during her birthday party; I couldn't stop crying, making everyone around surprised by my rawness.

I saw hope on their faces when I literally dragged them from their houses where they felt totally depressed, and took them for coffee so that they could see that life truly is beautiful. I saw faith when I coached the most hurt heart, showing them that there is light at the end of the tunnel.

I found out I had a gift.

Today, I am a transformational and spiritual coach, speaker and author. I call myself the Self-worth Seeker, True Identity Advocate, Femininity Ignitor and Sacred Space Keeper, a Creator of the Women and Girls Empowerment Movement, and the Real-life Manifesto of Authenticity and Rawness. Others call me the Earth Angel, the Oracle, and Inspired Spirit Coach.

What I call myself is less important than what I am trying to do in this world!

Today, I believe in myself like I never have before. I am here because I have a life purpose. All circumstances in my life, as well as the hardships and obstacles, have helped shape who I am, and my purpose for being here.

You, too, can truly believe in yourself.

I can hear you saying "Izabela, it is not that easy. I can't just believe in myself when I was told that I am not smart enough," or "I will never make it," "I need to have lots of money to invest," "There are so many people doing this already," or simply, "I will never be loved or beautiful." It is true that it is not easy, but you can do it. And none of the above statements are true.

I heard it every day. People who apparently loved me told me I was a piece of shit. I was never going to accomplish anything. I was stupid. I was poor. I was nobody. I was fat. My boobs were saggy. My booty was too big or ugly. I was too short. I was not athletic. I was not artistic. I was at rock bottom and would never get up. I should give up and return home to my parents. How could I possibly even believe I could make it work? My dreams and goals were the stupidest ideas. I was never going to be in a relationship if I didn't change myself. Nobody would love me for being the honest person I was – I heard it all.

I relate to how you might feel. At one time in my life, I thought there was no chance of me getting out of that cycle. I couldn't imagine the light at the end of that tunnel. Even worse, I could never imagine how it would feel to believe in myself.

I am here to tell you otherwise; *there is a way out of it.* There is that inner girl within you rebelling and screaming at you; "We need to get out of it, *we are superwomen,* we've got this".

You don't need to be a coach, a motivational speaker, a multimillionaire, a CEO, or a foundation creator to be a powerhouse and a wonder woman. You don't need all of that to believe in yourself and in your potential. You just need to be the way you are!

Let's get to work.

Let's get you from where you are right now to the self-believing and limitless woman you are meant to be.

- *Fear.*

Evolutionarily speaking, fear is a built-in system to protect us from dangerous situations such as fire, hunger, predators, or other life-threatening events. These still do exist in varying ways. They are just not the wild, uncontrollable fears they used to be. However, in today's world, in most cases, fears such as the fear of success, starting a new business, moving into a new country, or having a baby, and many others, are the ugliest "creatures" stopping us from moving forward and achieving beautiful things in our lives. They hold us back from believing in ourselves. They tell us what is not true, and they paralyze us totally.

How many times have you had the moment of wanting to do something new, something creative, or something that your heart has wanted for quite some time? And then the fear of judgment, rejection, or failure has crept in and you put a stop to it. After a while, you saw somebody else pursuing that one thing you wanted to do. All you thought then was, "Why didn't I even try?" Exactly!

There are so many things we want to do, and yet we let fear stop us from doing them. Think about all the things you could be doing if the negative stories and fear were not inside your head. It is time to stop that voice from limiting you. It is time to make peace with that voice. It is time to tell it: "I hear you, I know you want me to stop because of the danger of the unknown; I am going to do it anyway, because only then I can grow, achieve the things I want to, and become the person I am meant to be". *It is your time!*

Recognize all the fears that are stopping you from doing whatever your heart and soul desires you to do. List all of them, from the smallest ones to the biggest ones. Do not judge them. There are not "stupid" fears.

- *The list of fears.*

Place a tick beside each fear you see to be true. Look at each fear and really think about it. It is okay to have fears; these are a part of life, and they are helping you to reason, reflect and move forward. Ask yourself if your fear is holding you back from pursuing what you want to do. Is this fear relevant to your current situation? For example, being poor when you currently have a job is a fear that is not relevant right now. Rewrite the fear statements into stimulating phrases.

Be honest. I want you to be real and serious about it. This is not a place to blame the world, or whine about how crappy your life is. This is the moment to take full responsibility for your life and observe it for what it is. Be aligned with yourself.

- *Is this fear true?*

I truly believe that *the mindful chain of action* is to recognize, accept, forgive, act, and move forward. Those are the steps towards any changes you want to achieve.

You have already recognized the fears holding you back, playing their show in your mind and sabotaging your actions. Now, you want to take a moment to accept what it is.

- *Accept the fears you wrote and see them as the limiting factors!*
- *Accept that they are not true and see them through the lenses of hope, trust, and love!*
- *What are the other thoughts and doubts coming up for you now?*

- *Accept yourself as you are now–with all your fears!*

Put what you have just done into practice every single time a fear creeps into your mind. Create a morning or daily routine where you will focus on how your body feels. Is there any fear or anxiety?

Once you feel any uneasy emotions, recognize them and give them a name. By naming an emotion we state clearly what it is and we can proceed to questions such as, "Is this true? Why am I feeling anxious about that? Is this real?" Write down the answers. Look at those answers. See how the fear is simply limiting you and "protecting" you from the non-existent danger.

- *Affirmations.*

Affirmations remind you that you can do anything you want, you are in the process of creating the reality you want, and you can trust it because you are worthy, enough, and you believe in yourself.

Affirmations may seem very irrational at first. There is nothing irrational about them, though. You are simply retraining your brain from the one which was conditioned throughout your life when you felt like you were not enough into the one which believes that you are worthy, powerful, and unstoppable. You have nothing to lose, and a lot to gain.

The journey you are on takes time, effort, and work. Without the conscious decisions, being present, integrating those small practices into everyday life, and choosing to do the work every day, this may not work.

You are aware that it takes time and effort to finish a project at work. It takes time and effort to raise kids. It takes time and effort to build loving relationships.

It takes the same time and effort to uncover and rediscover yourself. But it is so worth it.

Isn't it beautiful to see your project being rewarded, your kids getting great jobs and marrying wonderful spouses, and your relationship being fulfilled and nurtured? In the same way, it is so magical to see yourself becoming the person you truly were meant to be–the person you are deep inside. Keep doing the work, step by step, and the reward will be outstanding.

I'd like you to write at least ten affirmations you can use every day. Write affirmations that can be used for different situations in your life: affirmations for self-love, time at work, around family and friends, when angry or depressed. Come up with ones for any situation and various emotional states.

- *My affirmations.*

Every chapter in this book finishes with mantras, which can be used as your daily affirmations, too. These are for you to use as often as you like.

- *Integration.*

The next step to self-belief is to implement small changes into your lifestyle, which will create the evidence of your wonderfulness.

What I found worked for me was lessening the amount of accomplishments I set for myself each day, so by the end of the day I felt good and I believed I could do it. Feeling good about myself was the evidence I needed to confirm so I could do it over and over again. For instance, if you are thinking about writing a book, start by creating 30-minute slots during the day to sit without any distractions and write. Simply free write the ideas you want to put on the paper. By setting a small goal, you not only feel accomplished, but also encouraged, and most importantly, believe that you can write a book.

It is as simple as it is hard. Gathering evidence may seem easy, right? Evidence is important for our subconscious mind. It reinforces that the job was well done, honored, and celebrated. Our subconscious learns to work at the same pace next time, too. It is the start of a successful pattern of your actions and subsequent results.

From my coaching experiences, and my own life filled with loaded lists of things to-do, I've learned that starting small is the key. It creates space for motivation, since you will not be as overwhelmed as with one big project all at once. Setting small tasks creates a winning mindset and the inspiration to do more next time. Anybody committing to do a particular thing for seven days a week, several hours a day with an already full schedule sets themselves up for just these results: failure and burn out.

However, making sure that you acknowledge what you've done, and that you are happy and proud of it, is the real work. And that's the ultimate goal–believing in yourself. Therefore, start small. Start with small tasks a couple of days a week.

I want you to be a winner. I want you to see that small steps actually make you more productive and focused than bigger and overwhelming steps. You can't get to the second floor by jumping from the first step to the twentieth.

Remember, go step by step. Make this your daily motto.

Before you take on this task, ground yourself using The Grounding Meditation "You Belong" (download here: https://mailchi.mp/67db2506b271/youbelong).

Take your pen and a journal, and create a plan. I want you to write down a list of at least ten small things you can do to reinforce that you can achieve anything you want and that you can believe in yourself. Remember, start small, and start slowly!

- *Let's create that boosting your beliefs list.*

- *Now take two things and start working on them.*

Take two small tasks from your list and schedule them in the first week to work on. Ensure these are tasks which can be accomplished within a day or two. Make space in your weekly schedule to work on those two tasks.

I don't only want you to work on them, but be fully conscious, present, and focused on the task. I want you to turn off the phone, go to a place where you feel safe and focused, and put your full attention into the task.

Afterwards, *I want you to celebrate it.* It can be done by simply acknowledging what you have done, stating clearly to yourself how you feel, how proud of yourself you are, and how you believe in yourself. Or it can be as sophisticated as getting yourself a gift–maybe a trip out of town or movie date night. Celebrate it!

The most important part is believing in yourself. Believe that you can do it again and again, because you just did it.

- *Write down your celebratory words to yourself.*

Create a habit of doing small things step by step, a couple days a week, and extend it as time progresses. However, do this only when you feel fully capable of doing it. Moving too fast may just discourage you, and this is the last thing I want for you. If you find yourself stuck, go back to the beginning of this chapter and create the plan over again.

Slow and small is the key here!

Let's schedule your week now!

Take the list of those ten "projects" you wrote down for yourself and pick two of them for the first week. Start today. Do not hesitate and do not wait. *Action and momentum are everything!* At the end of the week ask yourself:

- *How do I feel after the first week?*
- *How would I like to feel after five weeks of fulfilling all ten goals and gathering evidence?*

I encourage you to share your experiences with me and the like-minded women in the Authentic Wellbeing Facebook community (all links are in the back of the book) or privately with me. Let's inspire other women to take action. We all are starting small, and we all appreciate the help, support, and encouragement of others! Use social media as your support system, connecting with others and becoming accountability partners.

You can do this!

I believe in you.

In the next chapter, I am going to teach you how to forgive yourself and others, creating freedom and lightness in your life. You will find peace. Your alignment with yourself, your inner voice, and Inner Child will create a foundation in your life free of past, hurt and codependency. Your Inner Child and you deserve that!

Mantras
I believe in myself.
I can do it.
I am capable of doing this.
I start small and slow so I can succeed.
I am fearless.
I am unstoppable.I am limitless.

NOTES

NOTES

CHAPTER 3

I am at peace with myself

presence
   here I am
   with the universe
   with the body
with me
in love with breath
in love with emotions
in love with now

In this chapter, I am going to guide you as you find peace and alignment with your past and your Inner Child. I would love for you to be able to forgive those who have hurt you. It is time to find freedom and lightness in your everyday living, being, and loving-the freedom which gives you wings to fly and create the impossible. My goal here is to demonstrate to you that by achieving peace, you become happy in yourself.

I will show you how forgiveness can open up the doors to freedom from hurt and codependency.

Why don't you love me?

It was a dark, cold, and super rainy winter day in Boston - another long day at the lab, another day of living with a heavy migraine, and, ironically, another day of coming back home, to the apartment, where I so badly didn't want to be anymore.

I lived there with my husband. You would think that someone who is unemployed would be waiting for you at home, with a fresh warm dinner, cup of tea, and a sincere hug expressing how much they've missed you. However, I was coming home to an unclean house, full sink of dishes, lack of food in the fridge, and some stranger sitting on the couch watching TV - a stranger who didn't even raise his head to see who had entered the room or open his mouth to say "hi" to someone he had married just two years before.

Every day, after work, I was so tired that the only one thing I wanted to do was to go home and go to bed. Instead, every single time I approached my apartment I needed to find the energy to go around the next couple of blocks, postponing the most miserable thing - coming back home. Home was no longer the loving place it used to be.

I couldn't handle it anymore. After a few weeks of not saying a single word to my husband about the fact that I was hurting, I couldn't bear the thought of another quiet day. The pain in my heart was overwhelming.

I felt hopeless and had no idea how to make someone love me.

I felt betrayed by God because this was not what was promised to us when we got married. Wasn't marriage and love supposed to be forever and ever till we die?

I felt empty. I would never wish for anybody to feel what I felt or to be where I was then. The ignorance from someone I loved so deeply was painful. The coldness in his eyes, if he decided to even look at me, was freezing to the bones. His look expressed how disgusted he was by me. There was just hate in his expression. I could feel his desire to kick me to the corner so I didn't exist.

I broke the silence. I asked if we could talk. And the answer was very clear. I would have to be extremely dumb to not get it. He turned around with a smirk on his face. "Are you crazy or what? Do you think I want to talk to you, you piece of shit?"

This next moment changed everything in my life.

I ran up to him as he sat in front of the computer. I kneeled and grasped his knee with my hands. I cried so heavily. The tears, despite the dryness from crying every night for the last year and a half, were huge. I looked up at him. He didn't return my look. His eyes were looking at the computer screen, totally cold and calm, like nothing was happening. I managed to say just two sentences. "Why don't you love me? Please, I beg you, just love me!"

There are maybe just three people in the entire world who knew this story. And now all of you know the most shameful and vulnerable secret I have kept to myself for so many years.

Time passed by. As I am writing this, I feel compassion towards my ex-husband. I feel compassion towards myself, too. I also feel liberation. I forgave, and I let it go.

I feel empowered because I can show you that you deserve to be loved, too. You are meant to be at peace with yourself, loving yourself and forgiving those who hurt you. You are meant to forgive yourself, too. Only then you can be in total peace and alignment with yourself. It is only then that you will experience total freedom. And the best outcome of this work is that eventually you will feel compassion for those who hurt you, too.

You are safe doing this work.

The following tasks may make you feel vulnerable, but I would like you to know you are safe. Find a place to sit where you feel safe and comfortable. Give yourself a tap on the shoulder, and tell yourself how wonderful, brave, and strong you are. Remember, you are safe where you are. *You are safe to feel and express your emotions.*

Reflect on these questions:

- *Is there someone in your life who has deeply hurt you?*
- *How did you crave love from that person?*
- *How did you behave to make that person love you?*

If you need to, cry or scream. Find that safety zone right now and just allow the emotions to flow and be. Don't be mad at yourself. Don't try to explain yourself. Don't try to explain for the other person, too. Don't be a victim and find someone to blame. Don't judge yourself. Now is the moment to just be and allow the emotions to flow.

- *What are you experiencing now?*
- *Is it anger, frustration, sadness, calmness, or relief? Or something else?*
- *How does that feel in your body?*
- *Do you feel it in your stomach, belly, throat, or maybe somewhere else?*
- *How does that manifest?*

The four steps to finding peace within.

In order to be at peace with yourself, you need to integrate the following steps.

First, recognize your feelings, triggers, and uneasy emotions.

Second, observe the emotions. Start asking yourself what these feelings mean. Where do they reside in your body, and what are they trying to show you or teach you?

Once recognized and observed, move on to the third and fourth step, which are acceptance and forgiveness. These two are the hardest parts of the full transformation, yet the most necessary to make you free, light, and at peace with yourself.

Lastly, move on to creating the person, the space, and the world you have craved all your life. Those steps are covered in the next chapters, so stay committed to yourself and keep reading and integrating.

- *Recognize.*

Every one of us experience the moments when we feel triggered by someone saying just one sentence. We may feel some kind of resistance towards doing a task, when our inner guts are screaming "no, no, no." Other times, we may feel anxious, and maybe experience a lower belly ache. On the other hand, we may wake up one day with the feeling of fulfillment, empowerment, or simple joy, not knowing where it's coming from. Whatever it is, once you start experiencing it, recognize it. It is ok to not be able to name the emotions, but you may still be able to describe it.

- *Name the feeling you are sensing.*
- *Name the part of the body you feel these emotions in.*

I encourage you to practice this daily. Get yourself into the present moment. When emotions show up, name them. Do that EVERY single time you feel emotions coming. Stop, take a deep breath, and describe what you are experiencing!

- *Observe.*

Get curious about what you are feeling! Observation is very important, freeing, and invites playfulness.

Let's look at these two analogies.

Imagine that you are seeing a huge box that you could fit in. However, you are not in the box, you just see it from a distance. Imagine that this box is filled with your emotions. And you are outside of it. You observe them, you see how they interact, and how they show up and disappear.

Just like the physical distance between you and the box, your emotions are outside of you, and you are outside of them. They are not you. They just fill you in.

You get to observe them as the clouds on the blue sky, but they don't create you, nor identify you. And as the clouds can

69

be dark or white, or huge or small, the emotions can feel the same way: heavy, light, overwhelming, or freeing. The sky itself doesn't change. The person holding that huge Pandora's box is the same, too. Just as different clouds come and go, different things get dumped into or taken from the box.

Once you grasp this concept, you will easily move into statements such as "I am experiencing anxiety" instead of "I am anxious." We experience emotions and feelings and that is beautiful. If we weren't feeling, we would be dead. Every living human being feels. Every single emotion is there to show us something, to express the state of feeling at that moment. Just like pain tells you that something is hurting, the other emotions and sensations give you a clue about something going on within.

There is no bad or good emotion, either. All of them are here to make you more of a human who is capable of feeling, not just existing like a mindless zombie. All of them are experienced due to the reaction to the particular event or person. Once they show up, they bring *a lesson* for you to learn. The lesson is to recognize, accept, and learn from these emotions in order to forgive and move on, if needed. Some may just come and go. *This is the beautiful process of life transformation!*

So now, after you have recognized the feelings, I would like you to get more curious about them. Remember, stay outside of the box. The anxiety is not your name, the tiredness is not your label, the joy is not your identification. You are you, who is feeling all of these emotions.

How wonderful is the fact that you can feel but you are not the feeling!

- *What do you feel?*
- *Where in your body is the feeling located?*

- *What does the emotion that you experienced a minute ago tell you?*
- *How does this emotion make you feel?*

- *Accept.*

Hang in there. I know it may feel frustrating right now, or even overwhelming, to feel all of these emotions. In some cases, it may even cause heaviness, tiredness, or a headache. These are natural bodily reactions to the emotional release. Stay with me. I have got your back!

- *Can you accept that emotion now and not beat yourself up over it?*
- *Can you let it go?*
- *Can you understand that the emotion is a cloud which will pass through you, teach you a lesson, show you things to reflect or work on, and will go away?*

I would love for you to learn how to accept your emotions. *You are strong.* Remember, the Universe will never give you anything you and your body can't handle.

- *The thought converting process.*

I want to teach you a beautiful way to shift your mindset and overcome the anxiety related to the emotions you experience.

I call it *the thought converting process*. I also use it in the journaling technique and call it the same, *the converting journaling process.*

The technique is very simple. Once you recognize and observe your emotions, write them in one column on the left side of the page in your journal. List them one under another. You may want to use double spacing in between the lines. Then you move to the process of accepting what it is and converting those emotions into the emotions you would love to feel instead. Those will be written on the right side of the page.

Let me give you an example:

I feel drained emotionally.	It is ok. I am allowing all of my emotions to be.
I feel like I won't be able to handle it.	It may seem hard, but I'll give it my best!
I feel unworthy.	I am safe to feel that and I am enough!
Nobody loves me.	I am lovable and I am loved.

Now it's your turn. Look at the emotions you write without judgement. Remember, you can feel any of these emotions freely. You are totally safe to feel! Moreover, it is your birthright to be happy, joyful, fulfilled, accomplished, and loved! None of the emotions you are experiencing will take that away from you!

- *Let's get to writing.*

- *Forgiveness.*

There is an important part of you which just can't be missed during this process. It is crucial to connect with it in order to forgive.

It is your Inner Child.

I gave a name to my Inner Child. Her name is Izabelka (because in Poland the child's cute version of Izabela is made by adding "k," and this is the name my mom used for me). I encourage you to give your Inner Child a name, too. You can even find a picture of yourself at age 5-12 and put it in a place where you can see her. It will create a space of intimacy, personality, and connection between the two of you.

Inner Child work can be huge, and it can be so freeing at the same time.

There are plenty of resources on Inner Child work. Here, in this book, we will focus on reconnecting to her, listening to, and nurturing her so eventually you can love her the way she always wanted you to.

As you read in the Prologue of this book, my journey to re-discovering and reconnecting to my Inner Child was through a painful memory from my emotional and mental abuse by my dad. However, it was the most beautiful moment recognizing that there is that inner part of me, who wanted to be loved the same way as I did - the part of me who wanted to feel safe and at peace, just as I did. It was the realization of not being alone, having that internal "accountability partner" or a baby I wanted to take care of, was very grounding and reassuring.

That memory changed the trajectory of my life and the transformational work I was pursuing. And I can promise you, it will change yours, too.

The Inner Child work may be intense, sensitive, or painful. Don't judge yourself for it. Imagine that you want to reconnect with a child who just came to your front door. Do it at your own pace. The rush, force, and impatience will just create more resistance and repel what you want to actually bring closer.

Recognizing, observing, and accepting emotions is necessary to see what is actually missing within you that you are so badly looking for in other people.

What is it that you could give to yourself and your Inner Child?

I didn't feel loved in my relationships. I felt scared when I didn't do things the way my partners wanted them to be done, because I was afraid of them leaving me. I was giving up on my activities and hobbies in order to spend all my time with them. I was giving in so I could be loved. The faster I lost more of my identity, the shorter the relationships were. I couldn't grasp why this was happening.

Now I know that because I didn't give myself and my Inner Child the love we both deserved, I couldn't find it in the external world. *Begging for love from others was my Inner Child's cry to be loved by me.*

Let's dive into your life. Let's look closer at some situations, triggers, emotions, patterns, and outcomes.

- *Pick one to three things you and your Inner Child may be missing, but you are so desperately trying to find in other people.*

- *Once you recognize these, ask your Inner Child how you can find it without looking for it externally. How could you give them to you and your Inner Child?*

Listen to her, give yourself the time, silence, and space so you can seriously dive inside of your soul and listen to her. If you have a picture of her, look at it. I am sure this task may bring some tears, shivers, goosebumps, and resistance. It may bring some traumatic memories. Whatever you feel, it is ok and safe to feel. **You are safe!** Revisit it again and again.

This discovery will set you free so that you can move forward.

Once I knew that my Inner Child wanted to feel safe, I knew that by creating a safe space to feel and be for both of us, I could feel loved and happy.

- *What does your Inner Child need or want?*
- *How can you nurture your Inner Child now?*
- *How can you start loving her?*
- *How can you work with her so you both feel worthy, loved, and happy?*

And the most important part!

Forgive yourself for not taking care of your Inner Child for so many years in the past.

- *What are you feeling right now?*

The forgiveness of yourself is the first and foremost important thing before you can go out there and forgive others. Once you understand that all the abuse from the past was due to the others being abusive to their Inner Children, it will be easy to forgive. They didn't manage to listen and give their Inner Children what they needed.

It is crucial to know that forgiving others is not telling the world that what they did was ok. It is releasing the strong energetic connection between the two of you, so you can let go of the past, feel lighter, and move on. It is like disconnecting from a heavy weight slowing you down or limiting you, so you can gain your power back, become lighter and freer, and let go of what no longer serves you.

You may even find yourself feeling compassion for those who

hurt you. They didn't have the chance to see the triggers. They didn't know how to observe them and recognize what was missing within themselves so they could take care of it before they projected their insecurities onto others and onto you. They possibly did all they could based on what was available to them at that time.

Please, remember that: feeling compassion to those who hurt us, forgiving them, and letting go does not mean that their actions were OK!

It may all sound like it is an unachievable task for you right now. It all may be like voodoo to you, but trust me, it is so worth it.

Connect to your Inner Child.

It will bring you peace.
It will give you an internal confidence to feel loved and be love.

It will simply set you free - free of hurt, grudges, hate, and anger.

Being needy versus wanting things from life.

The entire process we just went through has an important message to embrace.

You are whole and enough the way you are. You don't need anything from external sources because you have all of it inside of you. It just requires recognition and discovery. That's why you are holding this book in your hands.

You know you are more than just being *needy*. I want you to see that neediness is not the path to follow. Needing something is when we feel empty, unworthy, and unfulfilled.

You are wanted and you *want* things in your life, on your terms, only so value is added to your own internal worthiness. This will make you even more unique and magical. Wanting is adding the additional tools, expertise, and values into something that is whole and totally worthy already.

Be the woman who wants things in her life.
Who wants to be respected.
Who wants to be loved.
Who wants to be wealthy.
Who wants to have a wild and intimate relationship.
Who wants to speak up.
Who wants to be her true self.

You are loved to the extent of how much you are loving yourself first.

In the next chapter, I am going to teach you how to get in the state of being in flow - that is, listening to your inner voice, following that voice, and trusting it. This releases all tension and slows you down so that you have the time and space to be creative in every area of your life. Doing what you love is the ultimate goal for you!

Mantras

I am safe feeling my emotions.

I am safe expressing myself.

I observe and accept my emotions.

My body is capable of handling the pain.

I forgive those who hurt me.

I love my Inner Child.

I am loved and wanted.

NOTES

NOTES

CHAPTER 4

I am in flow in my life

then your soul feels fulfilled
and your heart
cared for
and your body
respected
and you become
joyful
playful
aligned
and in flow

In this chapter, I am going to show you how to start expressing your emotions and feelings while honoring their presence, acknowledging them, and turning that experience into self-healing. Once you are comfortable with your emotions, you can develop deep self-trust and the ability to listen to your intuition.

I will show you how being in alignment with yourself can be freeing, releasing all tension, and slowing you down. This offers you the time and space to be as creative as your soul wishes to be in every area of your life.

I didn't want to live anymore.

I was never depressed as a teenager or even in my early twenties. I guess I was lucky, especially seeing and knowing that so many young people are being diagnosed with this life-threatening illness every year. The statistics are devastating. There are more and more young adults and even kids committing suicide. Depression, anxiety, panic attacks, fearfulness, and chronic stress are the leading causes of death in today's society, alongside diabetes, stroke, and heart attack.

Knowing that I was a part of those statistics in my late twenties sends a shiver down my spine.

I was a PhD student in Germany. I was in a relationship with my soon-to-be husband, who didn't want to move in with me for over three years. The loneliness of missing someone I wanted to be with and being away from everybody I loved was heart-breaking. The cultural differences, different family affairs or traditions around holidays, and my frustration in trying to create new friendships added to the loneliness. At the same time, my scientific project wasn't working. Eventually, I needed to replace it with a new one after almost two years of hard work, giving me less time to finish my degree.

Depression showed up unexpectedly. Suddenly, I preferred to stay in my room, sitting on the floor and crying, instead of going to the lab. I didn't want to hang out with friends and lab mates, despite the fact that I was a very outgoing person. I didn't see any change in my behavior until my boss called me into his office one day and asked what was going on. I knew nothing of depression and definitely had no idea I was depressed. After a few months of severe isolation, I went home for a Christmas visit. Then it hit me. I was giving up on my life. I was giving up on my degree, on my project, on my relationships, on my health, and on my dreams and goals.

Thankfully, with the help of loved ones, I bounced back.

But it was short lived.

A diagnosis of a mental disorder is something that stays with you for life, leaving and returning like a boomerang. A few years later, my "fresh" marriage was falling apart. The love of my life disappeared in a heartbeat, leaving behind overwhelming pain and scars.

I was strong enough to end the relationship, but not strong enough to not fall into the deepest hole of the depression anybody could ever fall into–trying to commit suicide.

I will remember that day for the rest of my life. It is a part of my life now.

It was a dark, grey, and rainy day. In the big apartment where I lived by myself, there was a bone-freezing silence. It was another day of questioning, "Why do I even exist?"

However, that day was somehow different. The silence was stiffer, there was no movement at all, as if all elements and atoms had paused. The darkness was comforting, and it made me feel like I belonged to it forever. There weren't any emotions. There weren't any words to be spoken. It was like being in space, or in a state of limbo.

The only little noise cutting through the painful silence was my own breathing. "Why was I even breathing?" That was the question. There wasn't any curiosity of who I was, what my life purpose was, or even how I could make it through anymore. It was simple to me.

"Why am I taking space in this world from someone who needs it more and can make real use of it? WHY? I shouldn't be here. I didn't deserve it at all."

I didn't want to live anymore.

There was no light at the end of the tunnel.

I literally saw myself walking slowly away from my life, confident that I wanted to go where there was nothing but darkness. I was calm.

I wanted to end all that nothingness!

Was I really that confident?

Today I don't think so. Maybe I was confident, but there was something else wanting me to be alive. I had no clue it even existed!

I managed to text goodbye to my boyfriend at the time, and I actually even responded to him a few times when he texted me back. I didn't know then that while texting with me, he was already driving to my place. It was only by the intervention of the Universe, all gods and goddesses, all angels and spirits that my boyfriend arrived at my place, pulling me away from the darkness.

It took me years to forgive him. I didn't want to be here, on this earth, and I blamed him for the fact that I still was.

The boomerang called *depression* kept coming back for almost ten years.

Today I am here to tell you that depression, anxiety, fear, or panic attacks are in many cases the choices we make every single day. There is a percentage of biological and toxic reasons behind mental illness, but there is a percentage that comes from within us. What we do with mental illness is our choice.

I truly believe that my depression ended at the moment *I decided* to stop using it as a tool to get more attention, be cared about, or feel loved and wanted.

I have never been medicated. I refused to treat my illness with toxic substances. I did not want to become dependent on them and not capable of dealing with myself. As a biologist, I could picture all the neuronal pathways and actions of how those substances were numbing the natural ways of my brain and mind to deal with it. I felt that the moment I started taking medicine would be the moment I no longer consciously cared about myself. I would no longer feel how I should naturally feel. Medication would cover the illness, not fix it. And if it ever showed up again, I would be dependent on more medication to cover it.

My decision to never take antidepressants was my own. I am not a physician who can tell you what you should take or not take, and I can only encourage you to seek help when you feel that it's harder than you can handle.

Deep inside of me, I knew that my illness should be treated by the practices of awareness and mindfulness so that I could consciously make the right choices and recognize the work that needed to be done within me. I knew that my body was capable of dealing with it. I wanted to live my life fully aware of my thought patterns and emotions, rather than being numbed by medicine. Once I recognized my own and my Inner Child's needs, and consciously decided to be happy every day rather than depressed–magic started happening! It was an interesting journey!

I finally recognized deep inside of me that I was meant to live this life; I wanted to be fully living it. I wanted to be fully aware of my bodily actions and thought processes, and to make decisions as me, not as a medicated person. I wanted to live life depression-free, totally and consciously aware of the fact that I was in control of it.

Was it that easy? Not at all. That was the hardest part of my entire life transformation.

[Update: Between when the book was written and publishing it some changes were made in my life. The hardships and my body's total lack of cooperation leading to a few life-threatening suicidal thoughts and attempts, led me to needing to make a decision together with my therapist and husband to support my healing journey by starting to take medication. Today I know that sometimes no matter how hard we try, we may need to become humble enough to grab onto any help possible to overcome that bump. And then the light at the end of the tunnel starts showing up.]

Fighting depression will always be a big part of my daily routine. I have to decide every day that anxieties and fears are the emotions I no longer identify with, but I recognize them, I observe them, I feel them, and I eventually let them go.

I no longer allow them to affect my day and my life.

The four steps to full alignment and flow in your life.

I shared my story with you to show you that life transformation, self-trust, and being free and in flow is totally achievable for every single person. Today, it may seem as dark as a moonless night, but the stars are still there!

Are you experiencing fear, anxiety, stress, depression, or panic attacks? I urge you to seek professional help when you feel it's too overwhelming to deal with it by yourself.

If you reached out for this book, that means that you want more from your life. I congratulate you on this decision!

This book is a tool for those who are struggling–a place of release. You are not alone. There are others with you. I am here with you, too. I am here to help you make this process easier, so you no longer spend your life in darkness, but start uncovering your light and creating the life you really want.

The process consists of four steps: recognizing the emotion, separating from the emotion, recognizing what basic needs are not met, and choosing differently.

- *Step #1: Recognizing the emotion.*

There are no bad or good emotions. All emotions are equal, and they are here to serve a purpose, which is to teach us and help us become more in flow.

It may sound easy to recognize the emotion, but believe me, I have had many experiences in my personal and client's lives that have shown this step is not actually that simple.

We are often ashamed of admitting what we truly feel. We are attached to old stories where expressing our feelings is considered weak or inappropriate. We have been judged many times, and most likely rejected even more often. When we speak up, we feel that we are demanding or behaving as though we are full of ourselves. Talking about emotions is seen as a taboo topic and a big "no-no" in society.

Communicating feelings and emotions is hard in relationships. Perhaps we've been told we shouldn't whine, we should make it work. We shouldn't talk, we should pull ourselves together and get stronger. We shouldn't cry, but rather find the solution. We are told to not express what bothers us, but instead numb it with alcohol, food, sex, gambling, social media, and who knows what else.

Fortunately, we feel. We know the feelings, we can name them, we can categorize them, we react to them, and we think about them. That makes us alive! Every single person feels every emotion we could ever imagine exists throughout our lives. There is not a single person on this planet who doesn't feel. And there is not a single person on this planet who feels the same way as another person about a particular moment, event, or thing in the same way, either. That makes you a truly unique person!

When you find yourself feeling anxious, or uneasy, and something is bothering you in some part of your body, just stop yourself. Pause for a few seconds, or minutes if you can, and try to recognize what's there.

- *What sensation do you feel?*
- *In what part of your body do you feel this sensation?*

That is your everyday task from now on. Ask yourself these questions listed below as soon as you wake up, on your breaks, on the bus, in between clients, before bedtime, and in bed. Ask them at any given moment to bring awareness to your body and your feelings and emotions.

- *What can you feel within your body right now?*
- *What are your feelings telling you?*
- *What is making you feel this way?*

Curiosity is the key. Curiosity and questioning open the door to a world of exploration, allowing you to observe and name the emotions you are feeling at that moment! Simply by being aware of what you are experiencing, you are recognizing that your feelings are temporary, and you have begun taking the necessary steps to regaining your internal balance.

- *Step #2: Separating yourself from the emotion.*

Emotions are like the clouds in the blue sky; they come and go, they get darker or lighter, and they change in heaviness and lightness; some bring a storm, and yet others will never bring rain. They don't define you.

The emotions explain what you feel and how you feel. They are the clues to what is going on within you. Just like pain indicates that something is hurting, cut, or broken, emotions indicate the underlying cause of their existence, too.

Emotions are not your name, identity, or label. When you feel anxiety, you are *not anxiety*. When you feel depressed, you are *not depression*. When you feel lonely, you are *not loneliness*. When you are joyful, you are *not joy*. Your name is Sam, Jessica, Pam, Sarah, Yvonne, Melanie. Your name is not depression, anxiety, joy, misery, happiness, overwhelmed, or calm.

This step is going to teach you how to see the emotions standing in front of you, not inside of you. Once you name them, you can separate from them.

The separation process is not a rejection process. We don't reject any feelings here. All emotions are equal, and all are needed for us to transform. We honor every single feeling, we acknowledge every one of them, and we accept them. But we don't identify with them. It is like another person in your proximity. You honor the person, you acknowledge them, and you accept that they are there. But you don't take their name and become them. You still hold your own identity and personality, your tag, and your name.

How do you master that process?

I developed a great tool which I call *personalizing emotions.* It is a simple act of imagining the emotion you are feeling as a person. Imagine that person in the same room with you, sitting across from you at the table, or wherever you are. Imagine talking to that stranger. The stranger wants to control you, take away your tag and identity, and wants you to become them. Obviously, your initial reaction will be to distance yourself from them. However, do it in a kind, respectful, and open way. No stranger will respectfully leave you alone without a fight or bad conversation when you attack them. What you reject comes back.

It is the same with emotions. Respect them, call them by name, and ask them kindly to leave you alone, or to give you space so you can see what is going on and get back to your life.

Tell them that you are truly safe and they can go!

The conversation could look like this.

"Hey fear, I know you are here. I can see you and I feel you. But listen, fear, I am on a mission to do something I truly believe in and I trust that it's going to be very good. I am about to go for it and start acting on it. I acknowledge your presence here. I know you are showing up to protect me from danger. But this is not a dangerous thing to me at all. I will be fine. I accept that you are here; however, feel free to leave any time. I am willing to see what you are trying to teach me or show me. In the meantime, thank you for showing up."

Practice this as often as possible. Start with small emotions and feelings about little things so you can practice the actual conversation without creating more anxiety. Start with separating self-trust from your emotions, giving yourself a sense of freedom, lightness, and happiness. Once you separate, you trust more. And when you trust more, the separation becomes easier.

To help you visualize this process, I invite you to do the Anxiety-Calming Meditation (download here: https://mailchi.mp/75fa222f2100/anxiety-calming). Observing, personalizing, and separating from the emotion is the main focus of this meditation.

- *Step #3. Recognizing what basic needs are not met in your life.*

I believe that every single time you experience emotions, or feel a particular way, you learn something. Therefore, you ask where is it coming from, or what is it trying to show me or tell me. At first you may not know, and that is ok. I assure you, it is totally fine if you don't know those answers today or tomorrow.

However, if you experience this type of resistance more often despite the work you put in, or for a longer time than anticipated, you may need to ask yourself why.

The more we force, the less we actually get out of this work. The more we "want" things to happen, the more things don't happen.

This work is not about putting in extra hours and working hard but instead about small steps every day, integrating the

96

lessons and tools you have, committing to showing up for yourself, and being aware and present. It is not about deadlines, results, and outcomes which you can report back to the world around you. It is about slowing down and allowing the answers to present themselves to you.

It is internal work, happening at its own pace. Keep going and allow it to work for you.

I am proud of you for still being here!

According to a very powerful motivational and transformational speaker of the 21st century, Tony Robbins, there are six core needs every human being seeks to make themselves feel fulfilled, happy, and successful (https://www.tonyrobbins.com/mind-meaning/do-you-need-to-feel-significant/).

There are personal and spiritual needs. The personal ones are: *the need for certainty, uncertainty, significance, love, and connection.* The spiritual ones are: *the need for growth and contribution.*

Every human being on this planet is driven by at least one, or sometimes a couple of these needs. In many cases you may find it hard to actually characterize what you really need to be fulfilled in your life. Sometimes the actual deep needs are under the layers of other needs we perceive as more important. I hope, after describing the needs, you will be able to clearly identify the needs in your life and know when they are met.

The need for certainty is met when you feel safe, supported, stable, that everything is in order, predictable, or in control in your life. On the other side, *the need for uncertainty* is fulfilled when you are in chaos, surprised, challenged, or excited, and you love the adventures and changes in your life.

The need for love and connection is the most common for human beings. All of us want to be loved and have a supportive tribe around us. You meet that need when you feel approved, connected, attached, stable in your family situation, and have the freedom to communicate and be yourself around your loved ones. For us, women, this need may be the most important.

The last of the personal needs is *the need for significance.* This need is met when you are needed or wanted, and when you feel you are special, worthy and important. That need, once met, gives you all the meaning and pride you need.

The last two core needs are the spiritual ones. *The need for growth* is very powerful. It is met when you invest into spiritual, mental, intellectual, and emotional development. It could be anything from implementing daily practices of meditation and spirituality, to flying across the country to participate in a 6-day business coaching retreat. You could take some extra classes to expand your knowledge to coach your clients better, or take CPR for children to be able to protect your kids when needed. Whatever gives you that feeling of pride, expansion, and fulfillment is meeting your growth needs.

Last, but not least, is *the need for contribution.* This need is fully met when you give to others beyond yourself; when you care, protect, and serve others–simply, when you are a servant of something that changes lives, even in your little community. You can serve your kids as a mother, and you can serve kids in Africa as a foundation owner. Whatever gives you that fulfillment, just simply do it!

As you can see, we all are craving something in life that makes us feel whole, empowered, motivated, confident, self-believing, and in the flow with our true self.

Let's identify what need, or needs, are not being met in your life.

- *What need did you resonate with the most?*

- *What need have you been trying to meet all your life?*

- *What is the core human need that you are trying to meet via the actions, or self-work you are pursuing here?*

- *What need being met gives you fulfillment?*

- *What need being met lights you up?*

- *What can you do to start meeting your needs today?*

- *Write down an action plan by listing one thing you could implement today, three things you could implement this week, and five big things you could start working on this year.*

Be honest! Be raw! Believe in yourself!

- *Step #4: Choosing differently.*

You have within your power the ability to choose how each day is going to be. You have the full power and potential to choose differently.

What do I mean by that?

Imagine those two scenarios in the morning.

You get up and the first thing you think is, "Oh, I am still so tired. Today is going to be hard! I need to get the kids ready, go to the store; oh, and I need to pay that bill because they may charge us an extra fee for late payment; how am I going to do all of it in just one day?"

The second scenario has exactly the same tasks to do during the day, however the person gets up and starts her day in this way. "Wow, good morning, what a great day. Thank you, Universe, for this gift and beautiful sunshine outside. Let's see what this bright day has to offer. I have got a few errands to do, which is fine. I should manage to do that, and I am hoping to have some time for myself later, too. That sounds doable and amazing actually. Hey kids, let's get going."

- *How did those two different scenarios make you feel?*

I sense that you simply don't believe that scenario #2 can be true. Many of my clients don't believe it. I didn't either, a while ago.

But today, I am here to tell you that it is true. The second scenario is how I rise most of my mornings. But truly, this is my morning conversation with myself, with the air, with the sunshine, with the Highest Self or the Universe.

It didn't used to be like that at all. I practiced the first scenario most of my life. And guess what? It did not work at all! So, one day I decided to choose differently. I had nothing to lose. All I had to do was change the conversation I had with myself every morning. I had to think differently. *And you can do it, too.*

I could write about all the benefits of positive self-talk, affirmations, and choices we make every day. There are plenty. However, I am not here to overload you with facts and statistics, but get you to take action! It is time to integrate the tools, because your time and life is precious. It deserves all the attention, effort and commitment you can give it.

If I were to tell you that this simple change in your daily routine will change your life, would you believe me?

Let's give it a try.

Start your day every morning with positive and encouraging self-talk. Do it for the first week, every single day. Be fully aware. Then write and journal the changes in your day's flow. Continue for another week – continue each week through one month. Before long, you will be doing it every day without realizing.

You can choose differently anytime and anywhere!

You choose the attitude that starts your day. Choose wisely!

I would like to congratulate you on the journey you are on. It is a beautiful journey of self-discovery, where you get to see what your true potential, power, strength, and identity are.

- *What does self-discovery mean to you?*

Self-discovery to me is the realization of who I am and why I am. It is the deep feeling of my own value, beauty, and worthiness without second guessing it. It is the moment when external approval and validations are not needed anymore because all I need, I can give myself. Self-discovery is reconnecting with the deep roots of my being, with my Inner Child and all that she needs and feels. It is the magical moment of being present, recognizing the desires of my body and soul and acting on them. It is being in alignment, at peace, and in flow with the nature of my true identity. It means being the unapologetic, vulnerable, sensual, and raw woman I am.

It sounds deep and very poetic. You may ask, do you truly believe that, Izabela? Is this just a metaphor or a real feeling? Who actually achieves that state of mind, body and soul?

My answer is clear. Yes, I do believe in what I write.

Moreover, I do believe you truly can accomplish this state, too. Once I experienced all of these beautiful places of my deep inner self, I knew I needed to share it with the world.

It is a journey, not an overtime quick fix!

I want this for you!!!!

We choose what we want to do every day, how we want to act, and how we want to feel. You can choose to feel peaceful, worthy, and beautiful, or you can choose to feel tired, unworthy, and not enough. You can go out into the world choosing to be confident or hide away from your true voice. You can choose to be playful, joyful, and happy each day, or miserable, disappointed, and angry.

You can have fun with even the most unbearable task, choosing to act upon your intuition and self-trust; you can choose to be in flow with your core values, what you want to create, and how you want to feel. Or you can choose to drag the task out over days and weeks, make yourself sick and reject everyone around you, blocking any way to solve the problems by only focusing on the potentially negative outcome.

I could list life scenarios like these over and over. We all have the same free will and right to choose. These are powerful tools which you are holding in your hands right now and every moment!

It is your choice every single day.

In the next chapter, I am going to teach you how to use that beautiful alignment and peaceful flow in your life to become the most confident and self-believing woman ever. The confidence you so desire is within you already. I am going to help you rediscover it again!

Mantras

I am in flow.

I am experiencing the emotion.

I can choose differently every day.

I choose happiness, joy, and playfulness.

I choose worthiness.

I chose to be confident and beautiful today.

I chose _____ today.

NOTES

NOTES

CHAPTER 5

I am confident

oh, poor thing
   feeling sorry for yourself
no
no
confidence is the key
confidence is the way
confidence it is

In this chapter, you're going to build up unshakable and undestroyable confidence in your life. I am going to convince you how being true and authentic buys you more confidence. I am going to teach you to speak up when it's needed and be quiet when it's not valuable to speak up. My goal here is to show you how saying "no" is the most loving response in many cases.

I am going to show you how self-worth and confidence build you up and create a strong foundation for every area in your life.

The immigration molding.

Boston Logan International Airport is a huge airport. It doesn't intimidate me, though. I have been to the big airports before: Frankfurt, Berlin, Munich, Hamburg, Amsterdam, Barcelona, Warsaw, Cracow, London, Edinburgh, Paris, New York, San Francisco, Chicago, Atlanta, Philadelphia, Denver, San Diego, and Miami. I have been to places.

When I arrived in the United States for the third time, it was not to visit, but to live and work here. The unknown was exciting, yet scary at the same time.

Relocating to the United States with just four suitcases, two for me and two for my (now ex) husband, and leaving our entire life in Europe seemed like a joke. I didn't know anyone in my new city. I had not even met my future boss or coworkers. I hadn't even seen the room we would be living in. Even a simple thing like calling a cab was foreign. However, thanks to the wonderful times we live in, I was able to check these things out online. I saw what Boston looked like. I spoke to my boss on Skype. I saw the description and picture of the place we would be living in. I wasn't scared at all.

I was confident.

I was excited. A new chapter had just opened up, offering huge opportunities and possibilities for both of us.

I have traveled and moved around Europe multiple times. Each time, I found it as an opportunity to see new places, meet new people, and create new connections. I learned something new, grew outside of my comfort zone, expanded the horizons, and enjoyed the moments. Traveling is the best memories-building tool. I saw the United States the same way–a new country, new culture, new friends, and new fun.

Learning the culture was the hardest obstacle, though. Understanding the value system and integrity patterns was the hardest part for me.

I call the process of learning how to live in a new place and culture *The Immigration Molding.*

It takes an enormous amount of open-mindness to embrace the differences of a new culture. It takes a huge amount of courage to accept the changes. It requires bravery to be yourself when you stick out so much. It also brings a lot of laughter when dealing with small nuances of daily life.

It takes a lot of confidence in yourself to not give up when differences become obstacles.

It takes a huge amount of tenacity to be able to stand tall and raise your head up standing true to who you are and your core values, and not allow your integrity to be compromised.

It makes you determined in pursuing things which are unknown, that is, the things which are outside of your imagination, comfort zone, and expectations.

What does confidence mean to you?

Let's talk about confidence.

Confidence is within us. It takes confidence to speak up,

express our feelings as they are, and to create boundaries and healthy relationships without compromising who we truly are. Confidence is the total trust in your own self, your abilities, your values, and your internal strength.

Confidence is not being insecure and projecting it onto others. It is not showing off despite the lack of self-worth within. It is not being better than others. *It is being secure and content with yourself.*

- *Does that sound tempting to you?*
- *Do you feel fully confident in yourself?*

- *What does confidence mean to you? List all of the emotions, characteristics, desires, and core values associated with the term "being confident."*

Rediscover your confidence.

We all live in a society where a lot of things are expected of us. As the oldest daughter and sister, I was expected to take care of my siblings. I was expected to give up a toy for the other kids. I was expected to always be proper, perfect, and a role model.

And that has impacted my life in adulthood.

I was expected to get the highest education possible, so I could keep being a role model and a provider. I was expected to marry a doctor or a lawyer. I was expected to dress in a modest way because I was seen and judged. I was expected to look a particular way because that indicated who I was. I was expected to be available any time of the day and night to solve the family's and the world's problems. I was expected to earn good money because only then I could be valued as worthy.

I was expected to forget my needs, desires, and sexuality so my husband was happy. I was expected to accept whatever pay came my way and forget my own value. I was expected to put a heavy mask on my face so I didn't show what my core values, feelings, or work ethic were.

I was expected to be fake in order to be loved.

I was expected to please everyone around me, but me!

- *Does that resonate with you?*

From an early age, women are expected to please everyone around them. We are truly people pleasers. We do have, by nature, the most beautiful qualities: we are caring, nurturing, unconditionally loving, and on top of that, extremely strong.

However, it is time to reevaluate our value system and understand one important aspect: *it is important and necessary to look after yourself first. Please yourself first. Otherwise, you are not going to be able to take care of your loved ones, if you are not well.*

Is it easy? No, it's not. Is it worth it? Oh yes, it is the most fulfilling accomplishment you can ever achieve in your life.

- *What were you expected to do and to be in your life? Be raw and honest. List **everything** you have on your mind.*

- *In what situations were you expected to shut up or put a mask on?*

- *When and where in your life did you behave totally fake, in order to be who others expected you to be?*

I wasn't always aware of my fake behaviors. As a child, you are taught to listen and be the way adults want you to be. You can't change their expectations of you. However, what you can do right now is bring total awareness to what exactly was expected of you, how you behaved, and how you were treated or judged when things happened. These things created wounds which need healing now. There is no confidence and an unconditional love of oneself when there is a constant internal battle, resistance, and regret.

In order to let that go, you need to recognize what was, accept it, and learn from it. The process I taught you in Chapter 3 applies to every single part of your life which needs attention and healing. *Recognize, observe, accept, forgive, learn, and move on*–as a fully healed, aware, and confident human being.

You have already worked on recognizing the situations and behaviors where you were expected to fake it. Now it's time to observe those behaviors.

- *In what situations were you expected to behave in a particular way? What way?*

- *Why do you think those expectations were put on you?*

- *How did you react to them?*

- *How did that make you feel?*
- *How does that make you feel now when you think about it?*

I encourage you to grab your own journal, because this is a huge piece of work that requires a lot of reflection and writing. Whenever I worked on this part of me, there were pages and pages filled in with my reflections, stories, and observations. Dive deep, painfully deep, and I promise you the transformation is just around the corner. As always, I ask you to not judge yourself. You are perfectly fine the way you are, and *you are safe!*

This work is not a one-time job. Give it time. Do not push

through or force it to happen at one time. It is integrative work, for every day of your life. It is a tool you can apply at any time.

I want you to be aware that weird situations, irritating people, awkward moments, and painful feelings are here for a reason: to bring your awareness to these, observe these things, and learn from them. *They are your teachers.* Once you approach situations that way, you will be blown away by how beautiful life can be, how much you already know, and how strong you are.

You have a huge amount of energy and strength to help you face any obstacles.

Get empowered by saying "no."

I would like you to answer these few questions, which will help gather the necessary tools for the work to come.

- *Think and list some of the obstacles in your life (from past or the present time).*

- *How did you overcome some of these obstacles in your life? Be specific as you name the actions, feelings, and reactions.*

- *When did you find yourself speaking up?*

- *What situations have you said "no" to?*

- *Did you say "no" to any requests where you felt you were being asked to compromise yourself?*

- *How did you feel afterwards?*

Read your answers again.

Saying "no" when you need to, protecting your space and time, being assertive in your community and at work, and setting up healthy boundaries are crucial steps towards creating confidence within yourself.

A life area where confidence and healthy boundaries play a huge role is relationships. These could be romantic ones as well as friendships and others.

As women, we are human pleasers. There's no doubt about that! I am sure that you have a ton of stories about how you gave up on your activities, opinions, favourite dress, or your beloved food in order to make another person happy. I feel you; I have been there, too.

It was overwhelming to some degree. It was creating within me indescribable feelings of irritation, aggressiveness, and anger–and I couldn't figure out where my feelings were coming from. I was internalizing it until I got so mad, hateful, and unhappy that people around me simply didn't want to be in my life. And I didn't want to be around people, either.

In many situations, pleasing others turned into a nightmare and battle within myself, where my mind spiraled up to the degree that I needed to leave a party. I didn't know why I was wasting my time on what was supposed to be a good time. I was trying to hang out with friends or a date, but I could see that it was not serving me at all.

I wanted to make people happy. I didn't know how to say "no," "I can't," or "I have other commitments." I didn't have enough self-confidence to stand up for my values and protect my space and energy.

I remember being on a date. This date was the "signature date" for the breakthrough I am just about to share with you.

This particular person had been asking me out for a long time. I tried to show interest, but I couldn't. It wasn't about physical attractiveness. It was gut instinct telling me he was just not right for me. However, one day I agreed. Oh well, I had nothing to lose, I thought. I could only get my doubts confirmed, questions answered, and my gut instinct proved right or wrong. The date ended up being the biggest waste of my time. There was literally not one single topic I could start discussing which would be kept going beyond two sentences. I stayed there for over two hours. I didn't know how to say, "Excuse me, but this just isn't working and I really need to go."

When I eventually left, I had an aha-moment. I couldn't lie to others because it is not fair to them and myself to agree to do something that does not align with my own values, energy, time, and myself. I needed to learn how to say "no."

- *Have you been in a situation you could clearly say has not served you at all?*
- *How did you feel?*

- *How did you feel afterwards?*
- *How did that serve you?*

When you give in and forget about yourself so others can be pleased, you do a huge disservice to yourself. You care, give, and nurture everyone and everything around you by tapping into your internal resources and energy. And at some point, those will be used up.

It is like a car; at some point it will stop due to a lack of fuel. You will, too. You will start internalizing frustration, irritation, and feeling that you are less and less worthy. Eventually your tank will empty and there will not be any energy to keep going. At that moment, you will find out that there is nobody to please, care, and nurture you – not because people are being selfish, but because the pleasing, nurturing, and caring has to come from within you. That has to be your priority!

This may be a hard concept to grasp. This may feel like a selfish idea. But this is an ancient truth: *you need to take care of yourself first before taking care of others.* You need to fuel yourself with the energy of love, worthiness, and confidence in order to give and help others. You cannot do something that requires so much energy when you are starving.

- *How do you care for others? List everything you do for everyone around you: at home, at work, at the park, at the club, or at church. Everything!*

- *How could you use at least five of those things and apply them to your own care?*

- *How do you care for yourself? List every single small thing you do for just yourself.*

- *How do you protect your time, energy, and space for yourself?*

- *How could you create, right now, three small things for your self-care?*

- *How could you schedule, right now, 30 minutes a week just for yourself?*
- *When would that be?*
- *What are some of the things you could do during these 30 minutes?*

Once you fill your "internal cup" with all things beautiful such as love, support, happiness, joy, worthiness, alignment, peace, and internal strength, magic will happen. The woman you have always wanted to be will grow. She will blossom from inside of you where she has been trapped for way too long–that confident woman, fully supported and loved by herself.

Commit to this step. It is your personal responsibility to put yourself first. I can't promise you any transformation if you are not wanting to give yourself that little care and love.

Once people see that you respect yourself, your time, and protect what is important for your own care and sanity, they will respect you and your boundaries the same way!

Tap within yourself.

The most beautiful part of all of this is that you will never again need any validation or approval of your worthiness and confidence from external resources. You will no longer crave acceptance in order to feel loved, because you will totally give that to yourself.

By external resources, I mean other people's approval, validation, permission or acceptance. This doesn't mean the approval of others isn't nice, but you do not *need* it to feel loved, worthy, and confident.

You *want* approval to be shown and given to you because you truly believe you deserve it. You know exactly what you are worthy of. You feel that you gave yourself the time, respect and love you needed and now you *want* to receive some of those extra bonuses from others.

Putting shiny, bright, royal red paint on an old car will not change the engine it is running on. By having that amazing deep connection with yourself, fueled by powerful care of yourself, you empower the "sexy Ferrari" that you are.

Is it easy? No, nothing in this book is easy. But everything here is worth every single minute of your time, because the person you are uncovering while doing this work is so powerful and limitless.

I'd love to meet you at the end of this journey and hear your story, because it is going to be huge!!! This is life changing for others, too.

By creating some me-time and completing self-care tasks, you are filling your "inner cup." It won't take long for this cup to be filled, creating a confidence that will have you sitting comfortably in silence with your own thoughts, emotions, and reflections, as well as around others without feeling less than.

The most beautiful and magical concept of self-confidence comes from being confident within and with yourself.

That is the moment when the true healing and transformation starts.

I would like you to start creating the beautiful habit of sitting with yourself.

- *Start by scheduling three to five peaceful "moments" a week without any distractions, for around five to ten minutes each. This is a time when I want you to do nothing.*

Yes, nothing, nothing, nothing.

And when your "nothing" moment is over, grab your journal and write whatever comes to you.

Isn't that the simplest task I have given to you so far?

I ask you to trust the process. I ask you to trust yourself. It may take some time, or resistance, or even frustrations. But this is your life journey. You are worthy of this "nothing" time.

I am saying "uncover" throughout the entire book, because the person you are meant to be is already there. You just require some care, attention, and love, as well as to be seen, to be heard, and to be able to speak up.

In the next chapter, I am going to teach you how to ask for help. Asking for help is an act of strength, worthiness, and confidence. Once you eliminate the judgment around asking for help, you will create an indestructible foundation for your true expression.

Mantras
I am strong.
I am aware of the life lessons I've experienced.
I am open and willing to observe and learn from them.
I accept myself.

I am fully confident in myself.

NOTES

NOTES

CHAPTER 6

I know how to ask for help

hurting your body
hurting your heart
hurting your beauty
hurting your little girl

I forgive
now
today
you and
me

In this chapter I am going to show you how to find the courage and bravery in your heart to ask for help. I want you to see how close you are to making the change that you've been craving. I want you to make a choice to commit to yourself and recognize that you are fully supported and provided for once you ask for help.

I will show you how crucial asking for help is to your healing and stepping on the path to your true identity! So, let's dive in.

Enough is enough.

"Oh, my goodness, this cashew butter is delicious," I told myself as I scooped another spoon of the nut butter. It wasn't the first spoon; it was actually almost the bottom of the jar. It tasted so good. Cashew butter was like heaven in my mouth. Don't believe it? Try it yourself.

Then it hit me – the realization of the fact that I had simply just shuffled into my mouth the whole jar of nut butter. "How could I possibly do that?" I asked as I started making my way to the bathroom. "No worries, girl, we will purge all of it and you will still stay slim," I recited in my mind.

That was such a relieving thought. I could eat whatever I wanted and then I could purge, eat again, and get rid of it again, and then repeat the cycle. I could be slim, happy, loving myself and have others loving me and, and, and... all these thoughts were spinning in my head! And the day was over. Tomorrow will be a better day.

Tomorrow is a new day. "Today is going to be a wonderful day," I recalled, as I did every day. My wonderful new day became the same as yesterday, as the day before yesterday, and as the last few months of my messed-up life. I guess that was my existence. Why did I even care? Purging seemed to be so easy. The only difficulty was when I went out, right? Not true. Purgers could manage in the most uncomfortable and unsuitable places. Because this is what matters most to them!

In November 2017, there was a day that started just like any of the others. I made an effort to be good. I ate what my body needed, feeling comfortable with every mouthful, knowing that I could easily purge afterwards. What I didn't plan on was getting depressed. Hitting rock bottom.

After yet another purging incident I went to a room where there was a huge mirror. For the last couple of months, I had avoided mirrors, hating what I saw. I didn't know what made me look on this particular day, but the image I saw this time wasn't the extra small "fat" girl but a person who was full of hatred – more hatred than anyone on this planet should be carrying.

The hate in my eyes was unbelievably huge. Words couldn't fully express the view I saw.

My eyes always change colors depending on the emotional state I am in. They are light blue when I am happy, or dark navy blue when I am angry, or greyish when I am tired.

That day they were beyond dark navy, almost black. I have never seen my eyes in such deep darkness. They gazed straight at me and didn't want to give up until I felt the hurt that they were showing me. They didn't blink, holding me to the deep darkness of hate they expressed. The lightning coming from them was blinding me. They reminded me of how hateful I was, how ugly of a person I was, and how worthless, miserable, and pitiful I was.

I wanted to turn my head away from the image I saw. However, I simply couldn't, as if someone was holding my head and telling me, "Look at yourself, look at who you have become, think about who you will be if you keep going along this path."

My body tensed, my hands and fingers squeezing so hard that my knuckles went white. My fingers became impatient, wanting to start scratching my skin. I wanted to hurt myself, feel the pain on the physical side of it. I wanted to rip my skin away and keep scratching until I bled.

On that day, the most magical phrase came out of my mouth.

"I need help. I can't do this by myself. Please help me."

I cried as I realized that my stomach hurt. I was still hungry, and I kept thinking that I shouldn't eat anything anymore. I cried because deep inside of me I knew this is not the way it should be. I knew in my heart that this was not the true me. Deep inside of me, I knew I had a mental eating disorder and that I could be cured.

I knew that there was no pill for it. The need for external validation, approval, or feeling loved was not helpful, either.

The first thing I needed to do was to decide that enough is enough. Then I needed to ask for help.

Asking for help.

It's simple, yet such a difficult thing to do.

If you have ever struggled with an eating disorder you will know what it is like to try a million solutions to find none that work. If you have ever tried to lose weight, then you know what frustration is. If you ever tried to expand and grow your company, you know how time-consuming that can be. You soon become overwhelmed with the systems and tools you've been using–and lost!

Let's dive deeper into yourself and search for answers. Grab your journal and write your honest answers to the following questions. Just write. Do not analyze. Do not judge yourself. Write from the heart. Write the first answer that comes to you.

- *Do you hate or dislike yourself?*
- *What does this mean to you?*
- *How does it feel to hate or dislike yourself?*

- *What do you live for?*
- *How would you like your life to look?*

- *What does being loved and accepted look like to you?*

- *Do you feel safe in your life?*
- *Do you feel like you won't make it by yourself and need help right now?*

I want to make sure that you know that *you are an incredible person.* There is something more out there for you than what you have settled for. Imagine right now that all is accessible to you. Please consider taking action now.

- *How does asking for help look for you?*

For me, it meant being weak, taking pity on myself, or not being smart enough to do it by myself. It took me a while to ask friends, family, or people around me for help. There was always a fear of rejection. The moment of being open and more vulnerable was scary to me. It meant that I may get hurt, again. The hesitation between being helped and being hurt is not an easy one and can paralyze anyone.

However, there were moments when I needed to ask for help. When I approached the situation being scared, sending low-energy vibes out, I usually got "no" as an answer. Did that mean that person rejected me? At first it did, but by looking more openly and without judgment at it, it usually meant the person either couldn't help or didn't have time.

Generally, people want to help others. That is our natural state of being.

When I approached the situation from the place of confidence, knowing what kind of help I needed and being open to any answer, I got what I needed and usually even more.

It is not an easy task. I am a woman and typically, as a woman, asking for help is really hard. We are known as multitaskers, those human beings who can be and do anything, anywhere, and at any moment. How mistaken we are.

Let me clear that one myth out of your life. There's simply no such thing as multitasking. Scientific reports have proven that your brain can not do two or more tasks at the same time. It can, however, switch very quickly from task to task. Despite that capability, we lose focus and lots of energy and the project is usually never accomplished in the period of time it would have been had we focused on just one task.

So, you can't do everything by yourself. *And that is OK!*

It is perfectly fine to ask for help. In the end, it feels rewarding, freeing, and empowering.

I would like you today, after you put this book away, to do one thing.

- *Think of one task, issue, or problem you need help with and ask someone to help you. Do it today!*

- *Journal how it made you feel to ask for help.*
- *What was the experience once you did it?*
- *How did you feel afterwards?*

It is fine if you feel constricted and stressed about asking for help. If you did, give yourself more time and space. Be kind to yourself. And try another day!

It is perfectly fine if you didn't receive any help, too. Not everyone has the skills and ability to help us with every task. If you ask with kindness, they may redirect you to another person who, or service that can help. They help you by being honest and not wasting both of your energies and time.

The very important part of this process is to not only overcome the fear of asking for help, but also to be appreciative of whatever you get when you ask. The more appreciation you show, even if the answer was "no," the more help you will receive.

You may have heard the saying that the more you appreciate your life and what you have, the more you are going to be provided for. This concept applies to everything in this book, including receiving any answers and help you asked for! We talked about gratitude in Chapter 1.

- *How did you respond to the answer you received?*
- *What was the reaction of the other person?*

Remember, you can't force anybody to help you. You can't expect anybody to drop their activities and tasks right now unless it's an emergency. You can't expect people to answer in a particular way or feel about the question in a particular way.

Therefore, it is important that you set yourself up for being open to either outcome. Say "thank you" for anything you get. Thank you is a high-energy and positive phrase when said out loud. It melts the heart of the most stubborn people. Maybe that person will return to offer their help later on.

We live in the world which is abundant with whatever we ask for. There are so many online and offline services, help groups, and coaching programs.

The biggest part of any success, personal or business, is to surround yourself with like-minded people–people who will be open to help, and who will create a space where you will feel safe to ask for help. I can't emphasize how crucial this is.

I would never be who I am if not for the great coaching programs I've found and the amazing support of the community. I wouldn't have built my business without interactions with wonderful people and brainstorming sessions. Any kind of success can't be accomplished without a support system and accountability.

- *What do you need help with the most?*
- *What is it that would bring you the most comforting feeling once you have been helped and heard?*
- *What would you be able to help others with?*

Write down what you actually crave help for the most. Be specific, and be honest. List areas of your life, desires, or questions. Be honest about how you can help others. We all have gifts. We all have expertise, wisdom, and knowledge we can share. When we genuinely help others, the service is returned to us. What we put out there comes back.

We tend to think of huge things. But look at your questions; some of them may sound simple, whereas others are not that simple. Remember, nothing is stupid or too simple. If the need for help is important to you, it is important!

So, do it. Ask for help.

Accountability partner.

- *I would like you to choose a person and ask them if they could be your accountability partner.*

Right now, a huge "no-no" may be screaming from your body. You may feel scared. Let me remind you that just a few moments ago, you went out there and asked for help. Did it hurt? Or was it relieving?

You have made the choice to make changes. You grabbed this book because you were looking for something else and something more. You have gotten to this point, so you are committed.

If this is a little daunting for you at the moment, it is ok. It is ok to put this book aside for a while at any time and come back to it later – but promise yourself you will not give up. Change is challenging and takes time.

So, go ahead, talk to somebody (who could be a family member, co-worker, or friend–anybody), and ask them for help. Find that person you can call your Soul Sister or Soul Brother. They are out there, waiting to find their partner, too. Be open, kind, specific, loving, and compassionate. Ask them how you can help them in return.

For the purpose of this work, I would love you to have at least one person supporting you. You will share the experience of this book with this person; this is the person with whom you will travel on this journey. Maybe you could gift them a copy of this book so that you are both on this path at the same time.

I promise you, it works magic.

You are worthy of any help.

You've got this beYOUtiful ♡

In the next chapter, I am going to teach you how to accept what is. True expression and true self-love come after full acceptance of what is right now. I am going to show you that acceptance is not synonymous with giving up and settling for less, but it is the first step to healing and truly loving yourself.

Mantras
I am worthy.
I ask for help because I love myself.
I am proud of myself for asking for help.
I am on the right path to my self-discovery.

NOTES

CHAPTER 7

I truly love myself

anatomy physiology genetics
all blamed for it
for too curvy or slim
for too tall or short
for too anorexic or fat
for too fit or lazy

number another number
how crappy does that feel

   however, look at her
how beautiful

   she is

In this chapter, I am going to show you how self-acceptance changes the trajectory of your personal growth. You don't need to love yourself yet, in order to accept yourself. Accepting allows you to move deeper into the healing of yourself, creating infinite possibilities.

Acceptance of yourself is the first step in the process towards loving oneself.

Girl, we need to talk.

"I am not perfect" I keep telling myself.

"Who are you to tell me this?" I respond.

"I am totally perfect, and if I am not, I can make myself as perfect as I want."

This is a conversation I often had with myself.

Do we need to be perfect in order to fit into relationships, society, community, and the world we belong to?

What does "perfect" actually mean?

In my country, everyone needed to look "perfect," especially girls. The competition started in early childhood. I observed many parents competing with each other about not only their wealth, but also about their kids' accomplishments and career paths. After every parents' meeting at my primary school, there was the judgmental "summary of worth" that Janette is better than me at math, Peter is stronger than me at his athletic performance, and Mary just got qualified to the regional language competition, but I didn't.

In high school, the competition went on even further. It was not only about my scholarly accomplishments, but also about my private life, like what I ate during the breaks. All of it directly indicated how slim, attractive, smart, cool, and worthy I was.

When I was a child and teenager, all our food came from our family's farm and garden. My parents were not only farmers, but also hunters and gatherers. My mom cooked literally everything from scratch. Because of that way of healthy eating, my metabolism was very good, and I never experienced being overweight. We always had a 3-course lunch and dinner.

The easiest way to have a home-made breakfast at school in my country was to prepare a sandwich. To have a few sandwiches for my '"second" breakfast at school, after already having one at home, was just fine with me. I was occasionally allowing myself candy, a granola bar, or even ice cream after school, but this way of eating was seen as something I shouldn't be doing. These limitations, rules, and expectations were put on me by my schoolmates. I wasn't fitting in. I wasn't dieting like all of my girlfriends. Dieting was fancy.

One day, at break, while I was so happily consuming my homemade smoked pork roast sandwich, looking forward to finishing so I could grab the homemade *pączki* (Polish doughnuts), a girl from my class approached me. She had a yogurt in her hand. She looked at me with deep jealousy in her eyes. Her voice indicated irritation and anger as she spoke to me. "How can you eat all this ugly food and not get fat?" My jaw dropped down. I looked up at her and all I could say was "I am sorry you can't eat what I eat." She hated me for the rest of my high school years. Not only her, but many other girls, too.

The more hate I got from their side, due to eating differently, the more I started eating the foods they ate. I couldn't tell my mom I didn't want the sandwiches she was making for me and my siblings. She put so much effort into providing them. She was waking up at least one hour before we did, so we could all have homemade breakfast and lunch boxes ready for us to take.

Instead, I was giving away my food and grabbing yogurt and salad in the school cafeteria so I could fit in. And in order for me to fit in, I needed to look slimmer than I was, so I could have girlfriends and most importantly, a boyfriend one day.

There were particular "requirements" one had to meet in order to fit in. One of them was to be the slimmest possible. My legs were too short, so I had to wear high heels in order to look taller and slimmer. My mom didn't disagree because she liked high heels, too. She took it as her daughter growing up and becoming a young woman. My legs were also big and athletic due to playing soccer all of my childhood. I could hide them by wearing very fancy wide pants or a long dress, and both were trendy at the time.

My breasts were a problem, too. They were too big for my slim and petite figure. I would often wear bras smaller than I should to try to hide them. By the time I got home my breasts were aching, but it achieved the desired social outcome.

Being liked and accepted was important to me. I wanted it so badly that I had to make it happen.

Soon enough, after eating in this new way, I started experiencing painful hunger. Just yogurt and salad all day wasn't enough at all. I was sneaking into the bathroom and eating my sandwiches so nobody could see me. It felt good at first.

My goal was to show off, to prove to everyone that I could fit in, and do whatever it takes to get to the place where I was accepted. However, one day some new emotions and thoughts showed up in my head.

Anger. Guilt. Self-pity. Fear. Self-discomfort.

I was questioning myself.

"What if they catch me?"
"What if I start gaining weight?"
"Why did I even eat that?"
"I am so angry at my mom that she is making 'ugly' sandwiches for me."
"I will never have a boyfriend."
"My body is so awful."
"I can't be looking like I do."
"I need to stop eating this food."

"Actually, why don't I even try to get rid of what I just ate?"

My eating disorder, followed by bulimia, began. Despite the fact that I was already size XXS, a very anorexic-like looking girl, I needed to make sure that I purged whatever entered my stomach that was not yogurt or salad.

I was never officially labelled as anorexic or bulimic as a teenager. It was not until the age of 32, the age of my fitness obsession, that I would associate these words with myself.

I remember the day these words became me.

It was two weeks after my bodybuilding and fitness competition at which I placed second. I was very proud of myself; I hadn't expected such an outcome. But I truly looked amazing!

It soon became an obsession to screen my body every time when I was leaving the bathroom. My plan was to keep my body in this ideal state forever. The magic number was 6.7%. That's the body fat percentage at which I felt beautiful and perfect, just the way I always wanted to look.

It didn't matter that my smart mind kept reminding me what I learned in college and at medical school. It didn't matter that my period was gone and I was at stage 4 of adrenal fatigue. It simply didn't matter that I could barely walk up the stairs or move around the workplace.

Nothing mattered because I looked fantastic.

It didn't matter to me how I felt, because all I saw was a fitness model in my own mirror. To hear compliments and words of validation about how I looked was fulfilling and approving.

Finally, someone loved me. Finally, I was seen as beautiful and looking perfect. Finally, I could see, on other women's faces, the same expression I was experiencing back in high school: jealousy, pity, self-doubt, self-hate, and enormous deep desire to look just like me.

Did that make me feel more loved? Yes, it did. I was so focused on the look that nothing else could exist. I had been craving to be seen and validated all my life. So now nothing and nobody would take that from me again.

That day, as I did everyday, I weighed myself. My heart jumped right away, and my blood pressure elevated. I was two pounds heavier and 1.9% body fat higher. That was a huge disaster in my mind. I texted my coach immediately crying about getting fat.

I am getting fat. How I hated myself!

My past memories from high school came back.

"Do I really need to go through that again?"
"Do I need to start purging again to keep my body looking so hot and sexy?" I thought to myself.

That was a tragedy for me.

My healthy lifestyle and holistic coach requested that I send her the most recent picture of my body. I stood there pinching every inch of my skin and seeing all that fat. After receiving the picture, my coach responded to me "Girl, we need to talk." So, we did.

And that conversation was mind and life-changing. It made me realize that I was mentally ill and obsessed with my body image. I realized something needed to change. I knew that my work with my coach needed to move to another level because I needed to start working on healing myself.

Let's draw the most beautiful picture of yourself.

- *Do you find yourself looking at your body and not liking what you see?*
- *Have you ever been at a place where it just doesn't feel good in your own skin?*

- *How would you like to actually feel in your own body?*

- *Do you think achieving an ideal body will make you happier?*

These questions may seem easy, but take your time and go through them a few times, and feel them. Tap inside your deepest desires and envision that body of yours–the body with perfect hips and breasts–the one with perfect legs, stomach, and shoulders. Envision the face with amazing cheek bone structure and shiny hair. Whatever the "perfect" body means to you, picture it!

Grab your journal or use the space below to write down that vision. Be as raw as possible. Nobody is watching, nobody is reading this, except for yourself. Draw the most magical picture of yourself.

- *What is the picture of the ideal and attractive body of yours?*

Describe how that body would make you *feel*.

- *Do you feel happy in your new body?*
- *Do you feel confident and loved?*
- *Do you feel accepted by yourself?*
- *Do you feel like that particular body will bring happiness and joy into your life?*
- *Do you feel that your family will be happier around you, too?*
- *Will those emotions make you feel motivated, driven, and empowered?*

The point of this exercise is to make you not only see the "perfect" body you would like to own, but most importantly, help you see how your vision of your "perfect" body creates emotions and feelings. Does that "perfect" vision make you truly happy?

I'd like you to take some time now and connect to your Heart using the Heart-Connecting Meditation (download here: https://mailchi.mp/38b92e82a19b/heart). It will help you to settle in the pictures you created for yourself in this exercise and see if they truly resonate with your deepest desires and your Higher Self.

In my case, despite the fact that I managed to make my body *look* beautiful and "perfect," I didn't *feel* beautiful inside.

I wasn't happy.

I didn't have any tools to help me look at myself, not only through the perspective of my physical body, but also through the lens of happiness. I didn't know how to ask myself if the numbers I was tracking actually made me *feel* happy and loved by myself.

They definitely made it look like I was loved by so many.

There is no time like the current.

The trap you fall into is that you strive to get the perfect body you have always wanted and whilst doing so neglect to think about other important aspects of your life.

All your life you are driven to perfection. That's human nature! You want to accomplish the best things so your parents, spouse, and others are proud of you. You want to have the most loving and respectful partner. You want to be a successful business woman. You want to be the greatest mom and wife. You want to look sexy and elegant.

You want to be at a place called "perfect and ideal" which in reality doesn't exist.

We tend to say very often, "When I get there, I will be happy," "When I lose weight I will be loved," "When I get to the point when I love myself, I will love everyone around me."

The thing is that there is no place that you need to get to. *This place is right here.*

I have seen so many women in my coaching programs wanting to get "there." Sometimes that place was so strongly envisioned in their mind, that it was hard to take their eyes from it. In these cases, I allowed the women to work on getting "there," just so they could see that being "there" wasn't making them happy at all.

Once you lose that ten pounds, will you be really happy? Once you get that partner, will you be truly happy? Once you move to another city, will you be enjoying yourself and your life? Most likely not, if the actual root cause of not loving yourself and being happy is not recognized and healed first. The root cause of that constant searching is within you!

The fact that perfection doesn't exist is actually very good. You are drawn back to the moment of now.

Bring your focus to yourself at this particular moment, and stop looking for the ideal picture. I want you to see every day as a moment to do something nice and beautiful for yourself. That way you will be able to get rid of all the hateful feelings towards yourself so you can create the most loving experiences for yourself.

Now we know, there is no "*there*."

When you are so focused only on one place, you don't see what is around you now. You don't see the journey toward the goal. You create the anxiety you experience every day.

The monkey mind starts its chatter again, "I gained two pounds, I'll never get there," "He didn't like me on our first date. I guess I will never have a relationship," "Why did I eat that cookie? I will always be fat."

I want you to do this simple and short task for the next seven days. Every morning, before getting into any activities, and before any other thoughts creep in, go to the bathroom and stand in front of the mirror.

- *While looking at yourself, start repeating these affirmations:*

Today is going to be a wonderful day.
I am doing loving things for myself.
I am doing loving things for those around me.
I am beautiful the way I am.

Keep looking at yourself, no matter what emotions you feel and no matter how ridiculous those words may sound to you at that moment. I want you to do that for two minutes, repeating these words, looking into your eyes, feeling them inside of you. If you feel angry, let the anger be. If you feel like crying, let the tears flow. Be yourself!

Every day you will feel slightly different; every day something new will pop up in your heart. It is extremely important to write these emotions down, and write them every day. Take this book and a pen with you to the bathroom and write down a few words about how you are feeling and what you are experiencing at that moment.

It is your choice to do loving things to yourself. It is your choice to repeat these mantras every time you are feeling anxious about your body. Decide for yourself. Commit to a better you!

- *Write here the feelings associated with this exercise every day.*

Day 1

Day 2

Day 3

Day 4

Day 5

Day 6

Day 7

Self-acceptance.

Self-acceptance is a very beautiful tool that helps you see who you are now, without judgment, and assists in getting rid of all self-rejecting thoughts. Without accepting yourself, you cannot change and heal. On the other side, you don't need to love yourself yet in order to accept yourself.

Imagine how your life would look if you were living the life where, despite the storms around you, you are still calm and aware of where you are. Despite the chaos, you know how to look at yourself and ask how you can nurture yourself right at that moment. Despite the stress, you are able to be kind and just simply OK with yourself and react in an anxiety-free way.

- *Let's do that one task now. Allow your imagination to flow.*

It may require your awareness, attention, and commitment. It is also amazing to see how quickly the shift can happen in your mind and body.

Body acceptance through breath work.

So far, we have looked at our bodies and seen them through our ideal vision. We made a choice to love our bodies the way they are right now using mantras and self-acceptance.

I would like you to recognize the times, throughout the day, when you feel anxious, a little uneasy, something is bothering you, or you feel judgement–either towards yourself or others. This requires awareness. Have your mind and heart open to it. Do not judge–"how crappy I feel," "Why is this person even here," "I will never be able to do that." Do yourself a favor–*do not judge!*

Once you recognize that little storm within you, I would like you to bring into it some attention. Step back from the activity you are doing. Take ten deep breaths, slowly inhaling through the nose, holding for a few seconds before exhaling slowly. Focus on your lungs expanding and the air going in and out. Focus on how *that* breathing at *that* moment makes you feel. Then return to your activities, observing how the breath work creates changes in your feelings and your body.

The last phase of this task needs your full commitment. Accept what it is, accept what came at that moment, and accept what showed up during breathing. Do not judge, do not be hard on yourself. It is about recognizing what your body is telling you without wanting to change it now.

- *How was your experience?*
- *What did you recognize in your body and heart?*
- *What beautiful or aha-moment did you experience?*

165

- *What was the obstacle you faced?*
- *Which part of this task was the hardest and why?*

Revisit the tasks in this chapter when you feel yourself disconnecting from acceptance, and instead judging and being hard on yourself. Use mantras in this chapter to help you see how amazing you are just now, the way you are!

In the next chapter, I am going to teach you how to embody your femininity. Being a woman is a true blessing. Being a woman is powerful. I am going to show you that your sensual, vulnerable, gentle, nurturing and caring qualities are your superpowers.

Mantras

I accept myself!

I accept the body I have.

I accept the life I have.

I accept the triggers and emotions I experience.

NOTES

CHAPTER 8

I am proud to be a woman

don't run away from it
feel it
it belongs to you
   it is you

you are beautiful
you are sexual
you are sensual
you are feminine
you
your body of magic
your body of wonder

You are a woman who is beautiful inside and out. The feminine aspect of your nature is empowering and attractive. Sexuality and sensuality are the most magical parts of being a woman.

Your Inner Woman is your true nature, true calling and true being. It is time to discover yourself through the lens of vulnerability, sexuality, sensuality, and desire.

What being a woman is not.

Have you ever been asked what you like about being a woman?

I have. Many times, especially as a public figure giving interviews to podcasts and magazines geared toward women. They like to ask that question a lot. I often wonder why they need to know that.

Sometimes I find myself irritated by it, and other times I feel offended or put on the spot, feeling judged regardless of what I say. Each time I am asked about that part of me I am left with uneasy feelings. I never know how to answer.

I used to be ashamed of being a woman. I felt weak, unworthy, and never enough because I was a woman. I thought that being a woman was weak and made me an easy object to use and abuse.

However, things changed at some point in my life.

Let me take you back to the beginning of the process of uncovering the woman I was meant to be. I was married at the time.

For me, marriage has always been a sacred connection to a person who you promise to love forever and ever, and they promise you the same. I married my fiancé after six years of being together, so I was sure we were meant for each other.

Long before dating my fiancé, when we were just friends and our families knew each other, I wrote in my journal that I would never like to date a guy like him. He wasn't as educated as I was. He wasn't working at all and relied on his mom's income. He wasn't as passionate and ambitious as I was. He wasn't the man my parents would imagine for their daughter. Ironically, I married the guy I didn't want to have in my life. "Love doesn't choose who to love," a saying common in Poland, played in my ears.

Our marriage only survived for 4 years. However, during that time I had the chance to understand what being a woman is *not*.

Observing my mom and other women from an early age, I knew I had to cook, do laundry, clean the house, keep his clothes ready for his work, additionally pay bills, and work my own job so that he could watch TV. As a woman it was not my place to speak up or be seen in crowds. Married women in some parts of Poland had to "disappear" from the public stage and hide under a veil covering their head. I was one of those married women, who hid underneath the veil in order to be accepted, taken care of, and loved. I also understood from my own stereotypical and traditional experiences, that I was there to make my man happy, whenever he wanted and needed me to. Despite my own feelings and needs.

My husband's work saw him working for a month straight before returning home for a few days. I quickly learned how to live by myself. I missed him and was happy when he was home. But things were weird each time and got even harder over time. Every time he came home, it was as though we needed to get to know each other all over again. This soon led to us fighting more often than being happy and enjoying ourselves. The emotionality, connection, and love I was craving was slowly disappearing.

However, no matter how offensive his words were, and how disrespectfully he treated me, I was always expected to meet his sexual needs. Get naked, take a shower, come to the bedroom, close the door, switch off the lights and lie down. Open my legs and pretend I loved someone who just emotionally showed me that I really didn't matter to him. He was ready, and I had better be, too.

I was being tossed all over the bed, so the position suited him. I was told that my bottom was too big, or breasts too saggy. There was always a part of my body which bothered him. If I spoke, I said the wrong thing, being labeled stupid. If I asked a question, I was expecting too much from him.

However, I still felt some emotional connection for a minute or two. I felt loved for a second.

I felt accepted despite some parts of my body not being the way they should be. I felt attractive even though it was dark, and we were covered by the comforter. I felt wanted because I was given that beautiful moment of intimacy by my (now ex) husband. I felt happy because I had missed him, and he was with me now. I felt peaceful because that was the only moment we didn't fight. I felt like a woman because someone still wanted to make love to me.

At least I thought I felt that way.

At the time, I felt like I had the most magical and intimate relationship on the planet. Oh, how mistaken I was!

As I "grew" into my marriage I began to recognize that there was a better way to go about being married. I started exploring my options.

One day, before our "romantic" and "intimate" night ritual, I asked my husband if we could make love in another way, a way that would make me feel happy and fulfilled. The words I heard destroyed my sexuality and sensuality for the next five years. His response was to ask me who the f*** I thought I was to ask such a thing. I was shattered. Any feelings I still had for him were depleted. I realized that there had never been anything there. All I wanted was to be loved by this man yet for him it was all about his satisfaction and fulfillment.

That night, during intercourse, all I could do was silently cry. I didn't feel loved anymore, nor wanted or attractive. I knew my bottom was too big, and my breasts were saggy. I was only there because I was his wife.

This was the moment when I realized I would be brave enough to say "no" next time. I did, and then the marriage just slowly started rolling downhill to the point when it naturally died. It took over a year and a half before I eventually said my last "no" to the man I so badly wanted to love me and that "no" felt so good. I bought him a one-way ticket back to his country. I didn't even tear up when he left the house, forever.

This experience allowed me to look at my womanhood and femininity through a totally different lens.

I hated the woman part of me. I couldn't accept it. Being a

woman meant constant period pain and blood, emotionality, being hurt and used by men, constant fighting for rights or equality, being less or unworthy, not having the same privileges, and more. I felt a deep hate. Hate towards being a woman and men using me.

It took over four years of self-work to rediscover and heal the femininity within me.

Aha-moment.

The question, "What do you like about being a woman?" has so much energy and power in it. When I took the time to really answer it, I felt an aha-moment.

Loving ourselves is important. So, what do I love about myself?

I love how loving I am, even of those who hurt me. I love how kind I am, even when I am faced with arrogance. I love how respectful I am, even in an abusive environment. I love how confident I am, even in the storms of life. I love how committed I am, even when things may not seem worthy at first. I love how powerful I am, even in the most critical conditions. I love how feminine I am, because I am gentle, sensible, nurturing, forgiving, and in the total alignment and flow with life.

I love how being a woman makes me feel–strong and beautiful. I love how being a woman reminds me of the limitless energy I possess within me. I love how being a woman is making me unstoppable. I love how being a woman makes me feel worthy. I love how sensual, sexual, and pleasurable I am. I love how vulnerable I am, knowing that this is my superpower. I know how unapologetic of my Goddess energy I am.

- *Can you relate to me?*
- *Is this how you feel, too?*

It's your turn to describe the woman you are.

- *I would like for you to write your own description of what you love about being a woman.*

Don't panic or get uncomfortable. We are in this together.

I haven't felt these emotions all of my life. The process of understanding and seeing the woman I wanted to be has been a journey through which I started discovering these qualities slowly.

Find a comfortable and safe place in your house where you can be yourself without being scared of someone judging you. Visualize the woman you want to be, and feel her in your heart and mind. Start with her physical appearance, and then go into her senses, actions, behaviors, and other details. Finish up with what she is actually feeling, allowing her emotions to run through your body.

- *Write the description of HER.*

- *What do you love about her?*

Congratulations! Now that you have met the woman you want to be, hold onto her. Take time each day to connect with her on a deeper level, discovering the feminine part of you.

The Woman and Goddess within you.

What does being a Goddess mean to you? Who is the woman within you?

Below I present to you a series of questions and statements. As you read these, answer them with as much honesty as possible. Focus on each one and commit to yourself. Do not judge yourself, but instead, embrace the woman within you as the beautiful and life changing experience that it is. Do not focus on negative aspects, qualities, or stories; instead, allow the beautiful woman that you are to evolve.

Remember, that woman is already inside of you. She just wants to have some attention, self-love, and safety so she can blossom. Let's give her space to do so!

Statement #1: She is loving, kind, and nurturing.

- *How do you see yourself at this moment of your life?*

- *What does being loving, kind, and nurturing mean to you?*

- *How can you be more loving, kind, and nurturing in your life from now on?*

Statement #2: She is loved.

- *How do you feel being loved right now in your life?*

- *How would you feel if you were told you are fully loved?*

Statement #3: She is beautiful inside and out.

- *What does beauty mean to you?*

- *What does inner beauty mean to you?*

- *How do you like to picture your inner and outer beauty in their most ideal state?*

- *How would you feel once you embody these qualities of being beautiful?*

Statement #4: She is in flow with her energies and her life.

- *Are you in flow at this moment of your life?*

- *What would that look like?*

- *How does it feel for you to be in flow with your life and energies, becoming the woman you want to be?*

Statement #5: She is strong and unstoppable.

- *What does strong mean to you?*

- *What does unstoppable mean to you?*

- *How would you like to embody those qualities in that Inner Woman of yours?*

- *How would that look and feel?*

Statement #6: She is confident and limitless.

- *Are you confident and limitless in your life at this moment?*

- *How does it feel to be confident and limitless?*

- *Who could you be once you are fully confident and limitless?*
- *What can you create once you are that woman?*

- *What one thing can you do today to become confident and limitless?*

Statement #7: She is powerful.

Being powerful is not about having control and power over others, or even you. Being powerful is knowing your own strengths and weaknesses, and leading a life of full acceptance and awareness. Being powerful may mean so much to you, and may involve totally different qualities to others.

- *What does being powerful mean to you?*

- *How does power look in your life right now?*

- *How could you create more women's power in your life and within you today and every day?*

Statement #8: She is sexy and sexual.

Being a woman is about embracing all of you, the most beautiful parts of you–your body, sex, pleasure and sexuality. You can feel safe here to express your deepest needs, dreams, and feelings. Be free and flow with the emotions and imaginations.

- *How sexy and sexual do you feel now?*

- *How does that express itself in your recent life?*

- *What does sexy and sexual mean to you?*

- *Are you confident being sexy and sexual?*

- *What does a sexy and sexual woman look like to you?*

Statement #9: She is attractive, seductive, and sensible.

- *How attractive, seductive, and sensual do you feel now?*

- *How would you like to express that when you embody fully the femininity within you?*

Statement #10: She is feminine.

The feminine part of you is something you can't simply deny. You are feminine within. As women, we tend to suppress our femininity to a degree where we are no longer aware of what it means. Femininity is everything that is soft, gentle, sensible, and flowing inside of you. Being feminine is being vulnerable and beautiful. The feminine part of you is forgiving, loving, and nurturing. Femininity sees strength in being vulnerable.

- *How feminine are you in your life now?*

- *How do you suppress or express these qualities in your life?*

- *How does femininity resonate with you?*

- *How does that woman you want to become express her femininity?*

Feminine and masculine.

When I first heard about these two types of energies, feminine and masculine, I had no idea how to respond. I associated masculine as something to strive for, and feminine as being weak. I didn't want to think of myself as being vulnerable, or even worse, soft and gentle. That definitely wasn't going to give me the self-confidence and empowerment I wanted to have.

I thought to myself that nobody would see me as a person worth hiring as a coach or pay the money I am worth if I am soft, emotional, or sensitive. I wondered who actually "invented" femininity. As you read earlier in this chapter, being a woman was something I rejected for many years. Finding out about femininity, and my reaction to this phenomenon, had me convinced that my rejection of my Inner Woman was correct.

I perfected how to embody all masculine characteristics: being strong, goal-oriented, organized, perfectionistic, idealistic, a hustler, and a hard worker. I was strong on the outside, and ashamed of my weaknesses on the inside. I was all perfect on the outside, and a total mess on the inside. I was a hard-working and hustling business owner on the outside, but totally lost on the inside. I was wearing masks that perfectly fit any situation I was in, which made me an ideal partner, coach, and friend on the outside, but I had no clue who I was internally.

The more I pushed away and squeezed all my deep desires,

dreams, feelings and emotions, the more miserable, lost, and unauthentic I felt. I wasn't self-aware enough, so I wasn't able to recognize it. It took me a little longer to come back home to myself. But when I did, oh gosh, what an aha-moment that was!

Dear Woman, dear YOU. It probably all sounds a little magic, or total voodoo to you right now. It is normal to feel discouraged from time to time, but I am here supporting you.

Let's talk a little more about what feminine and masculine mean, how you can embody these two parts and what can you do to make yourself feel truly and authentically proud of being a woman.

Every human being possesses both energies, feminine and masculine. There is no defined percentages of how much you need to have of each of them. It is all about the balance between them rather than emphasizing a particular one. The stage you are in your life may also determine which characteristics will be more present or dominant.

For instance, at work you may exhibit more masculine characteristics. Those are great to lead and manage people, organize the teams, and make sure everything is done before a deadline. Totally understandable. However, the masculine part is very tiring if in dominance all the time. It requires you to be strong, precise, well organized, and almost perfect at all times. Nobody can live like that for a long time. It drains all the energy out of you; it doesn't matter if you are a woman or a man.

That's why coming back to a place of peace, alignment, self-care, awareness, and being in flow with yourself is almost necessary to stay sane. That is the feminine side of you.

You may ask now, "Oh well, how do I do that?" Or even more, "I can't show the feminine qualities because my team won't respect me"; "How do I incorporate that in my busy work schedule?," "When I show vulnerability to my partner or family, they will treat me as oversensitive and emotional."

I know what you mean.

It takes a huge amount of compassion, trust, and courage to see femininity as a superpower rather than weakness. It all starts by slowly implementing awareness into your life practices and showing all of it in an authentic and real way. It takes time, effort, and mindful practices to integrate it into your life. You were born as a pure embodiment of femininity. You just allowed yourself and the world to suppress what is inside of you. It took me years to do that, so give yourself credit and accept that work to heal takes time. But you so have got this, beYOUtiful!

There is no magic or fast solution for making change. By engaging in the activities in this book, you have been introducing new concepts to your body, feeling them, observing them, being with them, so eventually you can see how they are shifting your energy to a more authentic you. You have begun to uncover what was covered by so many years of expectations placed on you.

Miracles happen every day!

Let's get to it. Grab a pen. It is time to uncover your masculine and feminine sides. List all the characteristics you have heard of or are aware of.

Be specific, e.g. I am very organized, however that creates a home with lots of restrictions, anxieties, and fights about little messes.

- *What do feminine and masculine mean to you?*

- *How do you embody these two sides of you?*
- *How do they show up in your life?*

- *How do they impact your life?*

Now I'd like you to read all of it out loud as many times as you need to.

Can you see both feminine and masculine characteristics in you?

It is only when we see the two that we are aware of how beautifully aligned they are, or how they are not. And that is totally OK. They create the authentic and real you; the powerful and intuitive, organized and in flow, strong and gentle, loving and loved person. Once you recognize both sides within you, you know how to connect them so they become your allies. That acceptance of both qualities, feminine and masculine, gives you an enormous tool to navigate your life in any direction you want.

You will feel connected to yourself in the most authentic way.

I clearly remember the first time I felt truly connected to

myself. I found myself enjoying small things throughout the day. I felt calm and safe in my body because I trusted that I was whole and worthy. I felt connected when I saw a great piece of art or heard a wonderful instrumental piece of music. The most beautiful moment of self-connection was when I looked at my naked body, and I could softly touch it and admire it. Sometimes it was giving myself a special tea, or making a delicious dinner.

For many of you, working and busy women, a moment of doing nothing, or taking a little break between tasks just to lay on the floor and daydream, might be what you need to connect. For those of you who work from home, putting on nice clothes and some makeup from time to time may give you a beautiful feeling that allows you to connect to your true femininity. Moments of deep breathing, reconnecting with presence, or feeling what is, might be a nice tool to become connected with oneself.

Be raw and authentic here. No shame, no judging, no limits!

- *What does the intimate connection to yourself look like?*
- *How does it feel?*

- *Write down at least ten things that make you truly and deeply connected to yourself in the most intimate way possible.*

- *What could you do now to make yourself feel truly and authentically proud of being a woman?*

- *Now read that list again, choose one thing that you can do today, and do it.*

DO not hesitate for a minute, because you can do it! You need to feel it now. You need to create that experience now for yourself. You need to get addicted to it now and for the rest of your life.

Join today this powerful, strong, loving, and energizing tribe of women–because the world needs you and wants you to be that person. I want you to believe in the qualities you possess and make them shine, stand out, and show your superpowers.

In the next chapter, I am going to teach you how to train your brain to create thoughts which will lead to the life you desire. You are the only person living your life. Only you can create this life using your mindset. The power of word and thought is huge. I am going to show you how to be mindful of this power and own it.

Mantras
I am truly myself.
I am whole.
I am worthy.
I am sensible and feminine.
I am beautiful.
I am loveable.
I am unstoppable.

NOTES

CHAPTER 9

I am the creator of my life

dig deep within
see
feel
and sense

you just created a
new you
real you

you just created
your world

In this chapter, I am going to show you that only you can create the life you want. I am going to teach you how to embrace the power of your own thoughts and how by doing this you create the reality you want. You are the creator of your own world; be mindful of it and own it.

I am going to show you how positive thoughts, words, and beliefs have the power to bring to your life exactly what you have asked for.

Getting to know who I am.

I see myself standing in front of a glass door. I have no clue what's hiding there. I find myself breathing deeply and heavily. I feel tears running down my cheeks. My sudden increase in heart rate indicates that I am excited. I am also afraid.

I stand there and all I can think about is that I am sick and tired of not knowing who I am. I feel deeply in my soul the unsteadiness of life. Luckily, there is that feeling deep inside of me telling me that there is a big change coming up.

I know that the door I see is the physical border between what it was and what it is going to be. I feel like I am about to leave something behind. I feel sad and sorry about the many years I am about to let go. But also, there is a curiosity about what it is going to be like there, inside that door. I feel brave enough to just go there, just walk through the door into the mysterious space and see what it is like. I am ready.

I am going inside.

I see myself reaching for the doorknob and smiling. I still breathe deeply. However, I don't hesitate anymore. I cry, with big tears. I am so ready. The mixture of feelings is not overwhelming anymore. I look at myself, then I look at the old me standing by my side, and I say "Goodbye, it was nice meeting you and being with you for all those years."

I push the door and it opens widely. I see the room; it contains very plain colors, greyish and white. Nothing extraordinary. Visually, the room has nothing to offer. The room is empty. Newly renovated, there are pretty lights and the smell of fresh paint. There are no emotions within the room. It feels spacious, echoing inside, just like nobody had ever been in there–like nothing had ever "contaminated" it with a single breath. It was as if nobody had ever stepped inside of it, nobody had ever said any word or expressed any emotions in there–a room of nothing. But, oh boy, how energizing it is inside of it despite that nothingness.

I feel that this is a room where new energies and emotions can be placed and start growing. My eyes are wide open. I hold my breath, looking around curiously.

I am comfortable here. It feels light and safe. There is no hustle, no noise, or any heavy or overwhelming emotions. There is no negative charge. There is no charge of anybody or anything, whatsoever.

I keep breathing heavily.

It hits me right away. I realize that this is my new space and my new place. I expected to see the answer to my question regarding who I am meant to be. Instead, I was given an empty room.

As soon as I realize why I am there, my Inner Child becomes happier. "No parents, no threatening, no fears, no abuse–can we just play?"

I get to design the interior, furnish the room the way I always wanted, bringing only the energies I want to be surrounded by, paint it in light colors to bring sunshine in, and decorate it with the most magical items. I am the creator of its look. I am the creator of my reality.

I am shocked, surprised, and overwhelmed with joy and happiness. I had hoped to see, inside of that door, some clues to my existence and life purpose. Instead, I am standing in a totally empty room, where I get to bring my life purpose, true identity, and personality with me. This was a place where I could create physically, mentally, emotionally, and spiritually the person I was meant to be. I am thankful for being given that opportunity, and at the same time, I am curious how am I going to make changes.

Do I feel fear? Yes, a little; there is the fear of bringing inside energies I don't want, or painting and decorating it in a way I won't feel aligned with and happy about. I am afraid I will judge my own masterpiece.

However, a few minutes later I become more confident. I know I will protect my new space, because it is my entire world and my life. I will make sure I ask every single person who steps in the door to leave their unwanted and negative energies on the other side. I will create such a strong and positive vibration inside the room that nothing and nobody will be able to discharge it.

Am I afraid of my own creation? No, I am not anymore. I can literally create my own world the way I always knew it was meant to be. I can make my room whatever I want it to be. There are no limits.

I get into action right away. I am anxious to start decorating, painting, adding plants, books, my art, altar, incense, and candles. It feels amazing. I literally have an opportunity to create something called "my life" and "myself" from scratch. Every single piece in this room is placed and organized the way I want.

I don't judge it. I fall in love with it every second. I nurture it and nourish it. I make sure it stays clean, fresh, light, and open.

The room gives me feelings of lightness, safety, love, and freedom. It is the place where I see my world through the lenses of love, joy, happiness, and pride. Pure creation.

206

I had this vision a while ago, when the fact that I am the creator of my own life and my world became obvious to me. At first, it sounded arrogant. However, once I embraced that fact, and started practicing creating small pieces of my life, step-by-step, day-by-day, I was confident that I am the creator. Just like in that vision.

All of us are given that empty room as soon as we are born. The room is yours to fill with the life you wish to live. The surroundings may influence the overall look of the room and the stories of others may fill it with different energies, but you are in charge and can redecorate it again, over and over. Even though the room may get cluttered and lose its beautiful look, you are still the creator of your life.

You need to take full responsibility for what it is at the moment, and start working on remaking it into what you want it to be. I believe every single one of you knows who you are, deep in your soul. You just need to peel off those layers of old paint to rediscover the beautiful "base color" of your true nature. You are truly beautiful, kind, open, and loving. That is your birthright – something you carry innately within you.

It's time to uncover the creator of your life within you.

The mind.

Let's start with the most powerful part of your body and at the same time, the most limiting one, which is the mind.

Your mind has the capacity to imagine, feel, understand, analyze, create, and visualize. However, it can also be the

207

most limiting force, sabotaging you, and being destructive to your beliefs, actions, and creations.

How is that possible?

The mind can visualize and focus on whatever you want it to, such as a beautiful house, loving family, and successful career. It can also very easily focus on the miserable job, negativity at home, the belief that you are not enough and that life has nothing to offer. The pictures your mind creates depends on you entirely, on what you believe now and what you want to believe.

Your mind is the most flexible organ, a phenomenon called brain and mind plasticity. Your brain creates neural pathways every single day, depending on what you are willing to learn. For instance, building a habit in your life is the process of reprogramming and rewiring your neural pathways within your brain.

Imagine the forest. There is a path through it that people always take. It is the same path you are going to take every single time, too. It is well defined, clear, and a safe way to get to where you want. It doesn't require you to pay attention to danger on the way or be creative in finding another one.

Life becomes like that well-established path. It becomes a routine. We go about daily tasks not paying attention to what we do or how we do them. We do things on autopilot because it is safe and doesn't require any thought or change.

However, this might be a habit you don't want to have in your life. In order to rewire your mind onto another path, you need to break through the logical, common, and "normal" patterns and step from the well-defined path onto a new one.

You can think of it as breaking through a thick forest to make a new path, which initially may be steeper to climb and may seem like the long way around. This may feel harder at first, but once you walk that path again and again, you condition your body to handle the hills, curves, and obstacles so well that they don't seem to be there anymore. This is how you create new neurological paths of the new habit, vision, belief system, or new story.

Your mind is the most powerful organ you possess. You can totally rewire it in any way you desire, which includes everything: the beliefs about your worth, life, relationship, or job; the visions of your future self and dream home, business, or partner; the attitude you adopt towards particular situations, events, and emotions–literally, everything.

There is one thing worth mentioning. Your mind is naturally more wired to feel and visualize negative things. The part of the brain processing negativity is bigger than the part processing positivity. Hence, there is hardship involved in rewiring the mindset towards positivity. We tend to somehow "always" feel negative, think negative, and see negative. It is called *negative bypassing*.

On the other side, that straight path in the forest may look easy, but it may not be joyful and happy at all. That curvier and steeper path, with more obstacles, may seem harder, but how enjoyable, adventurous, and beautiful could it become by discovering new views, new worlds, and new ideas.

You can train your mind. I am here to show you that you are the creator of your life, every single day. How? By making new paths in the neurological forest of your brain.

I love using my favorite analogy to show how society is living these days. I call it *the zombie lifestyle*.

Imagine a person who has been brainwashed and became a totally mindless person, following the particular and limited rules given to them by an invisible dictator. That person moves, behaves, thinks, and acts just the way he/she is externally created. That person doesn't think, create, or imagine. That person just simply moves as every other "zombie" person in the world. The opportunity to create something more is unattainable; the new paths away from the commonly used ones are forbidden, and the chance to be different is scary.

You and I live in such a society. We follow rules created within society. We limit ourselves by the stories which are not ours. We don't allow ourselves to grow because it would be seen as unacceptable.

Do you want to be free, unlimited, empowered, successful, and inspired, or do you want to live a "zombie life" where everyone around tells you who you are and what you can do? Or where you tell yourself that?

You are the creator of your life.

Start rewiring and training your own brain to serve you the life you want. You are unlimited in choices. You were always destined to live the life you deeply desire. Your true self knows what you really desire.

How do you do that in your life?

The language you use is the first important tool. Words can spark your mind and direct it onto the particular path you choose. Even if it doesn't feel real, start using words in the most positive, hopeful, and loving way you can.

When you think of your job, use positive and appreciative words to describe it. "I may not be doing exactly what I wanted, but I am thankful for having this well-paid job to support my family" instead of "I hate my job; I never wanted to do what I am doing now."

When you think of your future house, use powerful and positive words. "I am going to buy the house of my dreams and it will look like a cabin, with huge windows facing the mountains. I am working on getting the support I need to fulfill my dream," instead of "I am sure that I won't be able to buy that house."

When you think of the partner you want to date, imagine how he/she will make you feel, and what passions and things will they bring into your life. What will you be willing to share with them? "I am looking forward to dating a person who makes me feel happy and fulfilled. We are having so much joy and fun together, that I can't wait to share with him/her my passions and life," instead of "I need to date as soon as possible, because I am getting older and everyone is already telling me I may be alone for the rest of my life."

How much fear is in those negative expressions?

Can you imagine yourself being positive while saying those words?

Let's work on your language and self-talk.

Let's do some exercises, which will totally rock your self-talk and allow you to create the reality you want to live in.

Exercise #1: "I am" affirmations.

When I was told a few years ago about affirmations, and the way I would need to use them in order for them to have an impact on my life, I laughed. I couldn't believe that saying words could change anything in my life. How could an affirmation possibly make me stop being mad at the coworker, or angry at my boyfriend? How could they help me be happier if I hated my job or grateful for what I actually didn't have?

If that's you right now, I ask you to stop your doubts and give me a chance to show you otherwise.

When I was at the phase of total negativity, self-hate, and I didn't see a way out of it, telling myself that I was beautiful, successful or that I loved myself was totally irrational. Things changed when I was using slightly different words, which were still vibrationally positively charged, but gave my mind that moment to actually stop and reflect.

For instance, for the last few years, you may have struggled with weight and somehow it has gotten even harder recently to lose it. Telling yourself in that moment, "I am content with my body," or "I am loving my body" would just create a huge frustration and your mind will be like, "Oh really, I don't think so."

However, if you incorporate slight modifications into your sentence, such as, "*I am in the process* of feeling comfortable in my own skin," or "I may not be the version of myself I used to be, however, I am appreciative of recognizing it and having the courage to work on this part of my life," do you see the difference? Do you *feel* the difference?

When you use affirmations, it's not only the words that you use, but also the way you use them that matters. I am sure you've heard the saying that energy and vibration is everything. It is important that you *feel* what you are saying, so keep repeating it because you want to *believe* in it. Looking at yourself in the mirror adds to that moment the feeling of honesty, when magical things can be seen in your own eyes or facial expression.

How do you feel when you are talking to your friend and they avoid eye contact? Do you feel unheard, ignored, or maybe even sad? When you talk to yourself, look yourself in your eyes, too. Respect the person who is talking and the person who is listening, that is, YOU.

Let's create a list of 10 affirmations that you can start using today. Write affirmations for every area of your life. Write the most naturally sounding sentences, which carry love, hope, and belief. Do not use words that bring judgment, comparisons, or any deadlines and limits.

For instance, "I am going to be slim by end of this month," "I am the biggest enemy of myself, let me get to work," "I am slimmer than my neighbor," or "I don't want to be fat." You want the words to bring you hope, giving you butterflies in your stomach and creating a smile on your face when you say them. Remember, use the phrases "I am," "in the process of," and "yet." They give your mind permission to appreciate what your state is now and work on evidence and solutions to bring you to the desired state.

Let's get powerful here.

- *Write your 10 affirmations.*

1.

2.

3.

4.

5.

6.

7.

8.

9.

10.

You can use affirmation card decks to further help you bring into your life more affirming words. One of them that would accompany this book well is "The True Identity" Affirmation Card Deck, and another is the "Make A Wish" Oracle/ Affirmation Card Deck which you can purchase using this link: https://mailchi.mp/8e6018eb3456/makeawish.

Exercise #2: Mantras.

Affirmations allow you to change the way you think. Mantras, on the other hand, allow you to visualize your thoughts, bring emotions associated with particular words, and help you through the hardship at the moment.

Let me give you an example.

When I participated in a 12-hour overnight endurance event where I was asked to perform tasks nobody would ever think of doing, I had two options. I could chant mantras, or I could give up. I knew I didn't want to give up, and I would assume you are also not willing to give up on your life opportunities when obstacles show up.

During these endurances, I found the true power of mantras. I repeated over and over when I was alone in the darkness, "You've got this, step-by-step, let's go." On other occasions, I sang songs from my childhood which were deeply connected with positive and very proud moments. There were moments when just one simple word was the best mantra I could use, such as, "Step, step, step," or simply just counting my steps so I could keep moving forward.

I would love for you to think of at least five life scenarios where you have experienced or still experience hardships. Write them down and then think of at least two mantras for each scenario that you can start utilizing when that obstacle shows up in your life.

Writing them is only the beginning of the task. The next step is to start using them, or repeating them verbally or nonverbally when speaking loudly is not an option. Step back from the situation which stresses you and repeat the mantra you just wrote. Repeat it until the body relaxes, calms down, and your breath gets slower and deeper. Just keep doing it over and over and the results will soon be evident.

- *List your 5 scenarios and the mantras that you can use.*

1.

2.

3.

4.

5.

I am hosting powerful events, workshops, and practices in the free FB community group where we do Heart & Body practices. These are sensual body movements coupled with repeating the mantra to help integrate affirming words not only in your mind, but also, most importantly, in your body and system. You can join this group using the link:

https://www.facebook.com/groups/heartbodypractices/ or simply typing "Heart & Body Practices FB group" in the Google search. I will be honored to guide you through this process via practices streamed live that we do a few times a week.

Exercise #3: Intentions.

Intentions are the starting point of every dream and vision. Everything that happens in your life begins with intention. When you decide to buy a birthday present, wiggle your toes, or call a friend, it all starts with the intention of doing it. You intend to do the particular thing each time you do it. That applies to all of your needs, whether it is for money, relationships, spiritual awakening, or love.

Before you make that call, set up the intention. Before entering the conference room for a meeting, set up the intention. Before starting your day, set up the intention. Before serving the lunch, set up the intention. Before mediation, set up the intention. Before doing the homework, set up the intention.

Every act and action, when performed with the intention of your mind, is more meaningful, and will give you not only motivation to do it but also more enjoyment, awareness, happiness, or feelings of fulfillment, accomplishment, and pride. Even for the harder tasks, especially when you feel aggravated, set up the intention to show up as calm as possible so the outcome will please you in the end.

Intentions drive all actions in this world.

Next time you show up for an event or are dealing with a situation, take notice of your intentions. What messages are you giving yourself and others that are affecting your actions?

First, start just by simply observing what the intentions are and why they showed up that way. Once you see that, ask yourself the questions, "Is this how I want to show up? Is this how I want to commit to it?" If the answer is no, what will be your intention next time?

Be a person of integrity. Nurture your core values and show up authentically. Keep this in mind when you are setting up your intentions.

Use this space below to reflect on a few situations or events you recently participated in.

- *What situations or events come to mind?*
- *What was your intention and how did that intention influence the outcome?*
- *Could you show up next time more honestly and authentically?*

Exercise #4: Visualization.

Visualization is a fun and a very powerful tool to learn, practice, and use every day. It is one of the most meaningful ways to create your desired life, job, relationships, and wealth. It is aligned with the Law of Attraction and many of us have either done it or at least heard of vision boards.

However, there is a trick to it. Just creating a vision board, and dreaming and telling yourself what you want is not enough. Words are important - that's true. Being clear on your dreams and visions is important, too. But there are also two major components to it, which are overseen or simply avoided, yet very significant to the entire process.

To just imagine the objects, places, and things is not enough. It is *crucial* to envision *actual feelings* associated with your dreams–*the emotions* which you experience once those dreams come true.

- *Who will you become?*
- *What kind of person are those visions going to create?*
- *Are you willing to enjoy the process to get there?*
- *How are you living now and how is that already impacting your future self?*
- *Where are you now in your life and how do you feel?*
- *Are those feelings the same as the ones felt by your future self?*

The second thing is that in order for you to become that person in the future, you need to become that same person *now*. If you want to be rich, you need to be rich *now*. If you want to have a loving relationship, you need to look into your relationships with others *now*.

If you want your life and circumstances to change, you need to change *now*.

I used to say: "If I were rich, I would help so many people worldwide. I would open an organization, send money to charities, and so on." The change didn't happen until I figured out one of the most important aspects of human transformation.

If I wanted to change the world and my reality, I needed to change first and *now*.

The moment I started changing the world with little or no money in my life, within the community I lived in, with clients I had, then the real changes happened. Then the more I had, the more I could share with the world. Abundance creates abundance!

Start with yourself. Believe in yourself, and take full responsibility for your life and actions, creating your reality while being true and honest to your core values. This is a very important and magical step you can do.

Go ahead and create your visions. Start with a vision board of yourself and the feelings you want to experience.

For instance, imagine yourself having a loving family. Feel the emotions of being part of that family.

- *How would they make you a better person?*
- *What would they bring into your life?*
- *What would you bring into their lives?*

Then see if you can give all of that to yourself now.

- *Can you love yourself as you want your partner to love you?*
- *Can you respect yourself?*
- *Can you be committed to yourself?*
- *Are you a person with a strong work ethic and core values?*
- *Are you responsible for things or people in your life now?*
- *Are you the person you want to be in the future?*

The empty room I spoke of at the beginning of this chapter is an example of visualization. Start visualizing yourself, and the person who you are becoming, while getting access to valuable, external things. Create yourself first, and create your life first. Become your own reality.

This task is eye-opening and creative at the same time. It is also very enjoyable. Create your most authentic self. Dare to dream!

- *Grab your journal and list your dreams, desires, and visions. Express all emotions associated with them.*

And now write down what you can do *today* to make yourself feel that way. TODAY!

Start with the place you are at right now in your life and with what you have access to. Start with little things that you could apply in your life easily and immediately. We all have access to anything we want. We just need to be willing to see the opportunities and be creative. *Be yourself to the fullest!*

- *What could you create in your life to give yourself that experience?*
- *What would light up your life now?*
- *How can you bring that to your life, household, or community?*

Exercise #5: Expressions of your needs and emotions.

I love this part. I believe that this part is crucial for us women in many ways. We tend to hold a lot of our feelings close to our hearts. We are afraid to speak up. We hide emotions because we are afraid of judgment. We don't express needs because we are afraid of rejection. We don't ask for help because we don't want to be seen as weak.

Expressing your needs together with your feelings has enormous power. It frees you from the perception that you are less than others, or whatever you need or want to say has no meaning and is not as important as the needs of others.

Being able to express your needs is life-changing. It may take some time, though – especially if you were told for your entire life that it doesn't matter what you need or feel, it only matters that all those around you are taken care of.

- *Have you been told that you are selfish when you take some time for yourself?*
- *Have you been told that others are more important than you?*
- *Have you been told that you are not the center of the world?*
- *Have you been told to stop focusing on yourself?*
- *Have you been judged for taking care of yourself?*
- *Have you been told that you are too sensitive?*

It is time to rewrite those stories which hurt your true identity and worthiness.

First of all, *you are very unique and special.*

Second, you are worthy and enough just as you are. You deserve to take some time off for yourself. You deserve self-care. You are not selfish when you care about yourself, filling the love cup, and making sure that you are well before serving others.

"Self-care is not a privilege, it is an obligation," as one of my mentors said.

The biggest disservice you can do to yourself is to not take care of yourself first. This applies to moms, single women, busy women, and women with lots of time to themselves already. You deserve at least 15 minutes a day to yourself to do whatever you desire and charge your batteries.

There is a very common analogy of self-care to the oxygen mask on the airplane. You are told to put the mask on your face first, before helping others, including your own kids. Why is that?

Because if something happens to you, you are not going to be able to help anybody else, including your own kids. The same comes with health. I hear so many women telling me that they need to take care of their parents, kids, and actually everyone in the community first. And at the end of the day, they are so exhausted that they have no energy to serve anybody else, including themselves. By doing that day by day, you are going to burn out. And you won't be able to help anyone.

Expressing your needs is not selfish. It is an important self-care practice. When you are expressing your needs, make sure you speak from a place of love, kindness, and compassion towards yourself and others. It can go as smoothly as, "Darling, I would love to take some time in the morning to sleep in because I haven't slept well for the last few days. Would you mind taking the kids to school tomorrow, please?" It can be as easy as, "I would love to call you and chat with you and catch up. However, tomorrow will be a better day for me."

Expressing your needs and emotions, as well as asking for help, will lead you down a path you do not yet know exists: the path of empowerment and enlightenment. On this path, you will not only be able to ask for help, express needs, and find time for yourself, but also create loving and respectful relationships with those around you. Once you commit to yourself with full respect and awareness, others will see you as a person of integrity and will respect you.

While doing the tasks below, don't find excuses for yourself such as, "But they need me," "How would they be able to do that without me," or, "That would be so selfish of me."

- *Let's start by listing things that you do to serve and please others.*

- *What actions and activities could be postponed, changed, or delayed so you have a little space for yourself?*
- *Can some of these activities be performed by others without you doing them?*
- *How can you implement a few little moments of self-care in between the activities of serving others?*

Think of small things such as going for a walk around the block, grabbing a salad and eating it in silence, taking the journal and pen to write some thoughts down, or picking up this book and rereading some of your mantras.

- *Write down 10 self-care practices you can start implementing today.*

1.

2.

3.

4.

5.

6.

7.

8.

9.

10.

You are worthy of every single minute you take for yourself. Just as you give your precious time to others, commit and give some to yourself today!

Exercise #6: The way you talk about yourself.

The language we utilize in order to expand our positive energy and create high vibrational conversations with ourselves and others is very important in creating the life you want. The way you talk about yourself has to be aligned with your affirmations, intentions, visions, and who you truly want to be.

If you want to be a kind and caring person to others, start talking about yourself with kind and caring words. If you want to be a good wife to your future husband, start talking about yourself as a woman worthy of that love, partnership, and respect. Be the walking and talking example of who you are meant to be.

Go out into the world. Choose a situation you are passionate about and share your thoughts and passion with others. Choose a person you would like to express yourself to and speak up. Choose something that has been bothering you for a few days. It may be that you are tired of cleaning up after your teen. It may be that you can't stay for overtime at work due to your other activities. It may be the partner you would love to go on a date with. You may have some thoughts which are eating you from the inside out.

Go about your day, with a full repertoire of affirmations and mantras, with the powerful awareness that you deserve some attention and care, and *speak up* about your needs and emotions in a kind and loving way.

- *Express yourself today!*

Celebrate and appreciate the fact that you did it, even if the answer was "no." Celebrate because you just made a step forward–a huge step out of the comfort zone you were in just a minute ago. Celebrate and tell yourself how proud and happy you are of yourself for doing it!

The way you express gratitude, love, and respect to yourself is how others will express it back to you.

In the next chapter, I am going to show you that you are unique, special, and one in a billion. I am going to strengthen your mindset, so you can truly become the creator of your life and your authentic and true identity. You deserve to be the unique and beautiful person you are.

Mantras
I am truly beautiful.
I am the creator of my own life.
I am true and authentic.
I am worthy.
I am enough.
I am my own best friend.

NOTES

NOTES

CHAPTER 10

I am one in a billion!

I am the ONE in the entire Universe
I am the ONE with my skillset
I am the ONE with my life stories
I am the ONE with my qualities
my experiences are unique to me
and
I am ONE and whole

In this chapter, I am going to show you who you truly are. This chapter is going to help you see that you are unique, worthy, and enough just the way you are. You are not broken, you don't need to be fixed, and you don't need to rush to get there. You are true, real, beautiful, and authentic the way you are.

I want to make sure that you close this book seeing your real self, without masks, without hiding and blending in–your True Identity shining and sparkling out to the world!

You and I are miracles.

One day I watched the most mind-blowing TEDx talk ever. It was given by a very enthusiastic, powerful, beautiful, and influential woman, Mel Robbins (https://www.youtube.com/watch?v=Lp7E973zozc). During her talk, Mel illustrated how precious each human being is. She used the statistics where scientists calculated the probability of you being born the way you are right now, at this moment, with that specific genetic makeup. The results took into consideration the probability of your parents meeting, dating until they got married, having kids, and the right sperm meeting the right egg in order to create YOU. Dr. Ali Binazir took it even further adding the probability of your ancestors from the beginning of the first humans reproducing successfully in a way to create your great-grandparents, your grandparents, parents, and now YOU (https://www.businessinsider.com/infographic-the-odds-of-being-alive-2012-6).

That's a lot of numbers and calculations. The final number and "the probability of you existing at all comes out to 1 in $10^{2,685,000}$ — yes, that's a 10 followed by 2,685,000 zeroes!" He concluded his study by saying: "The odds of you being alive are basically zero. A miracle is an event so unlikely as to be almost impossible. By that definition, I've just shown you that you are a miracle. Now go forth and feel and act like the miracle that you are."

I wanted to share that scientific information with you, because even for me, a scientist, it was unbelievable to read the article.

I wanted to share it not only because it left a real blueprint inside of me, after which I never doubted myself being a miracle anymore, but mostly because you deserve to see that you, too, are a miracle.

Some of you may say that those are just numbers. That is true. This chapter is going to give you examples and tasks that help you see that you are a miracle just because you are here; you are alive, you exist, and you share the life you have today with people around you. Your very existence influences others. Your soul, heart, body, and mind, and your wonder and beauty are the miracle called you.

This concept may be overwhelming or unbelievable right now. Creating a resilient mindset and strength will allow you to embrace those words with a full heart and openness.

You may be a product of your ancestors, but you are the creator of your own life, a one in a billion destiny.

Embrace it with your full heart and soul!

How to never stop being a miracle.

I am going to help you create habits and beliefs that will not only make you aware of what a beautiful miracle you are, but also make sure you never stop being one.

Habit and belief #1: Own it.

There are no doubts that you are here on this earth for a reason. The place you are at is the perfect place for you right now.

Think about it this way. Imagine some of your major experiences which made you just the way you are and created the place you are at. Think about where you would be right now if those things had never happened.

It is not a reflection of what you regret. It is a moment of awareness of events in your life that happened for a reason. Every single one of them, good or bad, was necessary in order to bring you to where you are now. None of them were bad or good; all of them were important and perfect lessons to go through and become who you are. If you see your past as a school with different subjects, lessons, and tasks, you will realize how much you have learned and how rich your arsenal of wisdom and knowledge is.

I invite you to own your life in every form. Own your successes and failures. Own your happiness and sadness. Own your accomplishments and rock bottoms. Own your emotions and feelings. Own your decisions and choices. Own your reality and experiences. Own your beauty and identity.

Own it all together. Own it because all of it created that beautiful flower you are now.

No matter where you are at, at this moment, you have a wonderful awareness of where you were and the most empowering tool in your hands–the choice of where you want to be and who you want to become.

OWN IT!

Your particular purpose is yours alone. You own it. Only you possess the gifts you have. Is it a gift to raise kids, be a teacher, a pastor, an influencer, a wife, or CEO? Whatever it is, it is yours.

Own it!

Own your gifts, own your talents, own your callings, own yourself!

Write down the experiences, life events, gifts, accomplishments, failures, and anything that comes to your mind that created the person you are. Write it in the column below, giving yourself space to associate each of those experiences with the outcome–what happened afterward, what would have happened if things had gone differently, who you became, what you learned, and how that influenced your life afterward.

No regrets and no judgment here–just be real, honest, and kind with yourself, as you have been throughout this book!

Be specific. Take your time. Keep adding events and experiences as you think of them throughout the day, week, or even month. Come back to this task as often as you want to.

Remember, you are just the way you are supposed to be today, here and now.

Own your life!

- *Let's get this out.*

Habit and belief #2: Nurture it.

How would you treat the most beautiful plant in your house? How would you care for the most precious jewelry in your possession? How would you talk to your best friend? How would you spend time with the person you deeply love?

I would assume you would care about those things, nurture the friendships and give time, space, and love to the relationships you are in.

Let's turn this introspectively.

- *How do you treat yourself every day?*
- *How do you care for yourself?*
- *How do you talk to yourself every single moment?*
- *How do you spend time with yourself?*

We never see ourselves as the miracle we are. We never see ourselves as our best friend, or a beautiful body that deserves to be cared for and nurtured. We know how to give all of that and even more to others, and we are so damn good at it. But when it comes to ourselves, we often say "Why do I need to do that?" or "I don't have time for that," or even worse, "I don't deserve that."

It hurts me a lot seeing that "phenomenon" being so deeply embedded in women's lives. We dislike ourselves more and more. We find excuses so we don't need to care for ourselves.

We run away from our feelings. We are afraid to speak up. We hide and blend in so we don't feel like we deserve to be loved. We feel weak because we are gentle, sensitive, sensible, and vulnerable. We are avoiding beautiful femininity because we need to show off and be "strong." We are never happy about ourselves and constantly looking for a magic pill to solve the issue. We think we are broken and we need to fix something that actually doesn't really need fixing.

In reality, you are whole, full, and complete just the way you are. The only thing you need to do is to uncover that person from underneath the layers of the past, trauma, abuse, negative self-talk, old stories, and belief systems; come back to the realization of the innate beauty, strength, power, and energy you always possessed; and just be the real, authentic, and true version of yourself.

Sounds beautiful, doesn't it?

This is what we are here to do. This is what you have been doing since the beginning of this book. Every single page in this book is a reminder that you are great the way you are. Believe it!

You are a beautiful flower and jewel, so let's get real and fully commit to self-care practices.

Self-care applies to not only your physical self, but also to your mind, soul, heart, and body on an emotional, mental, and spiritual level. It is the practice of taking care of yourself when things are wonderful and when things are not that pretty. During those times, self-care is even more crucial for your well-being.

I want you to write down ten self-care practices for yourself. Remember to include your physical, mental, emotional, and spiritual self. Each life component is equally important! Having a haircut will not replace the negativity in your mind. Being loving to others will never replace the self-hate acts towards yourself.

Nurture that beautiful flower that you are today, and tomorrow, and forever!

- *Write down 10 self-care practices for yourself.*

Habit and belief #3: Flourish it.

The life you are living is priceless; own it! Take time to care about the beautiful, precious, and miraculous self you are.

It is time to grow. Growth is not only the expansion of your physical capabilities, your education, or your bank account. Of course, all of that is important in our physical world, too, to live, prosper, and be able to provide for ourselves and our families. However, the growth we are talking about here is *the expansion of your mind, heart, and soul.*

Growing your *mind* is not only educating yourself, participating in seminars, webinars, and self-improvement classes, but also your mind expands when you train it by creating nurturing habits in your life. The neural pathways are branching out by working on mind plasticity via the language we use. Creativity and visualizations are great ways to grow our mindsets, too. Acquiring new skill sets is an important part of becoming more aware and mindful of your amazing skills and talents.

What are five things you can start implementing in your life today to grow and expand your mind? Pick one and add it into your weekly schedule. Choose another one for next week. Continue until all of them become a part of your life. Don't stress about adding them all at once. Go slow. Be patient!

Celebrate when one of them becomes a daily habit.

- *Write down the five things to grow and expand your mind.*

1.

2.

3.

4.

5.

Growing your *heart* is as important as expanding your mind. I am not talking about an endurance training regimen to increase and grow your heart to perform better. I am interested in creating life experiences that will make you a person with a huge heart. Loving, caring, sharing, helping, empathizing, inspiring, motivating, appreciating, forgiving, listening, understanding, and giving back–those are the ways to grow your heart.

- *When was the last time that you sent a love message to someone you care about?*
- *When was the last time that you listened to a coworker in pain?*
- *When was the last time you called your family member whom you have had a conflict with in the past?*
- *When was the last time you took a relaxing bath in silence to rest and recharge?*
- *Have you recently forgiven someone who caused you anxiety?*

- *When was the last time you truly shared without expecting anything in return?*
- *When was the last time you stepped outside of your comfort zone to help somebody?*
- *When was the last time you told yourself that you are worthy, beautiful, and lovable?*

I could list many beautiful and tiny acts of pure love, compassion, kindness, and caring that you could do every day. Showing love, sharing magic, and being a beautiful role model is the least expensive tasks we can get involved in. All you need is your huge heart. Love and kindness are the cheapest, yet the most life-changing tools in this world–and the least used ones.

I want to share with you my life purpose statement, which we all could live by. I always finish my video episodes saying, *"Go out there and be love, go out there and love, today and now!"*

- *How can you love today?*

- *How can you share love today?*

- *How can you grow your heart every single day?*

Growing your *soul* is as equally important as that of the mind and heart.

When I speak of the soul, spirituality may be the first thing that comes to mind. This is a big part of the lives of many people in this world who are amazing influencers and very empowering leaders.

Spirituality is beautiful, magical, and life-changing. It is the most intimate part of your life. It is very individual. It is never wrong, bad, or incorrect. Spirituality is about doing whatever feels right for you and what is needed to align, empower, and drive your soul's energy to its highest level of vibration.

Spirituality is connecting to your spirit!

Don't let others tell you what is correct and how spirituality *should* work. There is no "should," "right," "correct," "wrong," or "approved" way. There is YOUR WAY.

Create a space in your house where you feel happy–a place that you will enter and it will put sparks in your eyes and a smile on your face. It can be just a little corner with an altar, maybe a few candles, flowers, some beautiful and meaningful ornaments, pictures, or decorations–whatever makes YOU feel connected!

If you want to meditate in silence, do it. If playing with oracle cards is the way you feel connected with your inner voice, go for it. If you simply want a safe zone to sit in, to not think but space out, just do it. Whatever it is that brings you to a place of calmness, stillness, lightness, and connectedness, do it!

- *What does your sacred space look like? If you have one, write down what you have there and what each part of it means to you. If you don't have one, turn on your visualization tool and create one in your mind–what would you like to have there? Why and how would it make you feel?*

To grow your soul also means to be mindful, aware, still, and calm. Be in the moment, look around and recognize small things you tend to skip. You may be so focused on your goals, hustling to get there, in a rush, full of stress and anxiety, that you don't see what is here and now. Many solutions and answers can be found exactly here and now, if you allow yourself to stop for a second.

Being in this moment may sound silly, unmanageable, or just not possible to do in your busy life. After all, we only have 24 hours a day. Surely, we can all afford two minutes of stillness a day.

We can afford five minutes longer in the bath in the evening to simply appreciate what we have in life and who we are. We can set the alarm clock to remind us to just be present. Step back from the task you are doing, go to the window, look out at the world, smell the fresh air, observe the birds, and see the leaves moving with the wind. We can all do that. There is no excuse for not taking a few moments out of each day.

My task for you here, as we approach the end of this book, is *to write a letter.*

Write a letter to yourself, just a simple conversation with yourself while you are standing in the nice place where you are, observing what is around you, and appreciating every single little thing. Use your senses to observe and recognize what comes to your attention and see the beauty in it. Start with your eyes, then use your ears, nose, touch, feelings, and if possible, taste. Notice things you may not have noticed before.

Witness the beauty and amazement in every little detail.

Take a piece of paper, or your journal, and write that letter. Take a moment on a work break or set an alarm to remind yourself. Just simply be with your surroundings, yourself, and your journal.

All that matters at this moment is this moment! *Enjoy it!*

- *The letter to myself.*

Can you see now how many opportunities the world and life give you every single day to expand your mind, heart, and soul–and shockingly all of them are for FREE?

These are the cheapest solutions to the most worthwhile outcome ever!

Habit and belief #4: Be it.

"Simply being" may sound like a hard task, but if I were to tell you right now to stop what you were doing and just take a moment to sit in a chair and be, how would you feel?

If I were to tell you just now, put this book, and all pens and highlighters down, and simply just be in the chair or bed you are now, at the moment of the day you are now, in the way you are just now, how would you feel?

- *Would you be uncomfortable or rather happy and excited about taking a break?*
- *Would you feel anxious about wasting your time or happy to have a moment for yourself?*
- *Would it feel like a big resistance or rather a joy of feeling aligned with yourself?*
- *Would it feel like a sharp pinch in your belly as your body tells you "no" or a warming flow of energy through your chest as an indicator of joy and relaxation?*

The simple *"just being"* in the place and time you are now and here is not as easy as it sounds. However, it is the most magical moment and place to be of all I have shown you so far.

"Just be" is the leading motto of my coaching programs, because this is the foundation and base where everything starts, happens, and falls into place. There is no yesterday, tomorrow, later, or some time. It is here and now.

If you can see who you are now, what your life is like now, what you currently have, what you are grateful for now, and how blessed and happy you are right now, then you are being the truest and most authentic self ever.

You are one, whole, complete, and unique right now.
You are beautiful, attractive, loved, and loving right now.
You are worthy and valuable right now.
You are in your prime moment right now.
You are in the perfect time and place of your life right now.

I understand that simply being and existing in nothingness can be the hardest task ever. But on the other side of that hardship lays pure magic and light.

My first attempt at "simply being" had me wanting to scream, shout, run away, and never come back. I felt very uncomfortable being with silence and anxious about being with myself. My mind was wandering to places I never thought still existed. My body was aching and itchy. My heart was so close to jumping out of my chest. My stomach was cramping. The first few times were a disaster, leading me to give up a few weeks later.

However, there was an internal curiosity that had me wondering what the other side of life looked like–no hustle, no perfectionism, no schedule, no deadlines, no comparisons, no lack in existence. Just simply being with no guilt of existing, and simple nothingness with no guilt that I was lazy, not productive, or not pleasing others.

The curiosity brought me back to it, and yet again, not even two minutes into simply being, the physical aches and pains started. But that two minutes of feeling nothing else but myself was heavenly soothing.

- *I want you to create two to three short chunks of time during a day when you will commit to the most important task, "just being" and doing nothing.*

Start really small, with the highest level of compassion, acceptance, and understanding that this is for you. Do it in a way that makes you feel comfortable.

Write down the feelings and sensations of the sessions where you managed to transcend to the place of beingness and nothingness and sessions which were not as successful as you might have thought they would be. Journal all of it, because one month down the road you will read it all again and realize how magical these moments were and how they have changed so much of your life.

Be curious, playful, and approach it with wonder and joy. Have fun with that!

Habit and belief #5: Make it a legacy.

You are one in a billion. You have talents, gifts, and skills nobody else has. You are a miracle. You are in the most perfect and magical place and time in your life. There is a reason why you are here and now. There is something in this beautiful world for you, just waiting to be taken in your hands and converted into an unstoppable, limitless, and empowering being–just the way you were born and meant to be.

This is called your life purpose, your path, and your journey. It is your life's mission.

It is your legacy you are creating every single day.

Whatever the name you give it, one thing is for sure:

You are meant to be your true and authentic self, choosing love and shining with the uniqueness and beauty you have within you.

Embrace it.
Accept it.
Feel it.
Be it.

Now go out into the world, and share the love and light you are!

Thank you for giving your heart, soul, body, and mind the nourishment it deserved.
Thank you for being your true, raw, vulnerable, and authentic self throughout this process.

Thank you for being the magic and love you are!

Mantras
I am one in a billion.
I am a miracle.
I am whole.
I am complete.
I am unique.
I am in the perfect time and place in my life.

NOTES

NOTES

EPILOGUE

I see a little girl.

She is running around in the park. Joyful and loud. Singing her favorite songs, the ones she always makes up. Jumping on the grass as she mimics the graceful baby deer. Waving arms all around trying to catch butterflies. Humming the music of her heart. Dancing and twirling in her pink and white dress, with random flowers all over. She spins until she loses her balance. She doesn't make anything out of it, continuing to have fun and giggle. Her curly hair flows with the breeze, creating an enormous halo effect around her head. She's having conversations with every flower she sees in the grass, and every tree she dances around.

The freshness and lightness in her moves are so obvious. She is united with the energy of flow. She shines. She radiates with joy and playfulness. She is alive.

She is real and fully herself. She doesn't care what others may say because she feels aligned with her own instincts. The childlike instincts that make her heart smile.

She is so innocent and precious in her being. Moreover, she is so powerful and confident in her body language.

She looks up at me with a smile.

255

I nod to her indicating that she is safe.

Safe to enjoy herself.
Safe to play and laugh.
Safe to fall and get up.
Safe to live and love.
Safe to express herself.
Safe to experience.
Safe to feel all the emotions.
Safe to be sensitive and sensual.
Safe to experiment.
Safe to get curious.
Safe to be.

She can see in my eyes the reassurance that I will be here for her and with her. I am not going anywhere. I've got her back.

She also can see that she is free and can live her life fully, authentically, passionately, and whole-heartedly.

She is whole and unique.

She is worthy.

She is gifted.

She is loved.

That little girl is me, little Izabelka.

I tell her,

"Go out there, girl, and play. Live, and live fully. Experience. Get curious. Try. Fail and get up. Feel all the feels. Be human and the divine being with human experiences. Feel the pain and joy, anger and passion, sadness and happiness, sorrow, and relief. Feel all of it. And I will be here. I've got your back. You've got to go out there and live your life fully. You can trust yourself."

And I let her be who she is meant to be!

I trust her…

I trust myself!

DANDELION

so elegant and graceful
letting the sunshine sparkle

so beautiful and attractive
spreading the love around the world

so light and free
sending joy to hearts

so delicate and vulnerable
yet embodying the power within

so transparent and authentic
showing beauty to the world

The dandelion is the best representation and embodiment of the values which I share with the world in my transformational, spiritual, and empowering life and work. It represents the values that I was driven by while writing this book–the values that I keep in my mind when I am creating content for you, the values which are embedded in my soul when I am serving you, and the values that warm my heart every time I share life and love with you.

This beautiful flower expresses the deepest set of qualities which I believe in, the morals which were born and grew with me, and the ideals creating every single cell of my being.

Vulnerability and delicacy

Transparency and forgiveness

Authenticity and openness

Gracefulness and elegance

Freedom and spaciousness

Alignment and peacefulness

Lightness and softness

Beauty and gentleness

Powerfulness and unlimitedness

Calmness and stillness

Love and energy

Uniqueness and wholeness

Value and worthiness

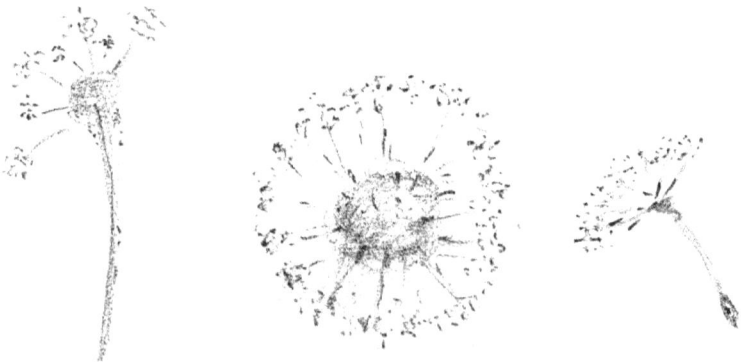

THE LETTER TO MYSELF

Dear Izabela,

I am so proud of you for creating the life you so deeply desire within you. It is a life where you are free of self-hate and aligned with your true self. It is an existence which is loving, kind, and compassionate; happy, joyful, and playful; it is real, honest, and authentic. This is a life in which you trust your intuition and believe in yourself and your life path.

I always knew I was meant for more than hustle, struggle, poverty, self-doubt, depression, suicidal thoughts, giving up, and feeling like a piece of nobody.

I knew I was here for a reason. I believed that there was a plan. I was brought here to create, fulfill, and share magic with the world.

However, I didn't know that the path to healing and uncovering my true self would be through feelings of pain; pain of regret, lack of forgiveness, abuse, sadness, anger, self-hate, self-doubt - *the pain*.

I didn't know that *the pain* was my superpower.

I didn't realize that no matter where I was and who I was there was a way through it.

I was meant to get through it. I was meant to stand here today with my book in my hand showing others the path I went through so they, too, could heal.

The healing happens through the pain!

Today I am strong, committed, and happy. I know I am meant for more. I am prepared for whatever lays ahead of me. There is everything I need already out there, and it always was. I just simply chose not to see it.

Today, I am the person I always wanted to become. I am standing on the other side of the pain, trauma, and past with a heart full of love, faith, and hope. I am truly me without the fakeness and masks I had been wearing all my life. I am vulnerable, kind, gentle, passionate, and joyful, sharing the magic of my true identity within.

Today, I am totally peaceful, aligned, fulfilled, trusting, loving, safe, loved, worthy, enough, complete, and whole.

I am prosperous and generous in every aspect of my life.

I am happy–here and today!

Just as I want ALL OF YOU to feel, too!

I love you, Izabela!
I love YOU, too!

ACKNOWLEDGMENTS

My deepest thank you goes to the Little Girl I call Izabelka, the girl who has been within me, since I was born. She never gave up on me, even though I gave up on her many times. I wouldn't be here today if I hadn't found her on that floor hurting and asking me to be with her. Thanks to her, I have been given the chance to change so many lives, including my own. Thanks to her, I am here, the servant of something freaking unstoppable!

My unlimited appreciation goes to my MOM, the woman who truly embodied strength, beauty, pain, and love, and the choice to truly be the woman she had always wanted to be. I have never seen anybody be so heavily abused, but still turn her face towards the abuser, opening her heart and loving them as if they never did anything wrong. I have never seen a more beautiful and loving human being treating others in such a loving way as my Mom always did and still manages to do. I love you, MOM!

I wouldn't be able to write this book without the encouragement of two people, my friend Krzysztof "Braciszek" and my sister, Aneta. I have no clue what they saw in me years ago, but they kept bugging me to start writing as soon as possible. Thank you for always seeing something in someone called "nobody" all her life, so she could become somebody today!

This beautiful creation wouldn't be here without every single person I have met on my path called life. Each of them has added a little more to it, so I could be here, just the way I am. The transformation was and continues to be magnificent. Thank you to every single one of you, the "bad boys" and "good souls," the small, tall, young, and old, the poor and rich, the mean and kind, the abusive and comforting, the friends and enemies, the loved ones and hateful ones. Thank you, all of you!

Thank you to all my clients I have had the honor to work with. They never ended up as only clients. They have become my huge family, an amazing crowd of beautiful friends, loving relationships, and an empowering tribe of human beings. This book wouldn't have made sense if it wasn't for YOU! I will cherish every single transformation in each of your lives, because it is what keeps me moving. Without the deep desire to change the world, by changing the life of at least one person every single day, I wouldn't have a reason to get up every morning, especially when it was as hard as hell. I love you all for the beauty, strength, wisdom, and love you brought into my life. I love you for the magical moments we shared and your empowering transformations!

I want to express my gratitude to every single person who donated to my GoFundMe fundraising campaign. Without you, this book wouldn't have seen the light of day, yet. It was an enormous financial and emotional support knowing that there are people out there who believe in me and want my book to be published as soon as possible. Thank you all so much!

I can't express in words how grateful I am for my bestie best friend, Ozanna. Thanks to her, I didn't give up multiple times. Thanks to her, MDSB was born. Thanks to her, beYOUtiful was born. Thanks to her, Authentic Wellbeing was rebranded. Thanks to her, this book has seen daylight, reaching out to its readers. She is the type of person you can text in the middle of the day crying and she will be with you and for you. You are a big part of this book, Ozanna. Thank you!

Last, but not least, a huge thank you goes to my husband, Kurt. I never thought I would find someone who would love truly unconditionally and be supportive without expectations. It amazes me how happy he can be living with a person who manages to have a breakdown and breakthrough at the same time, or cry and laugh in the same day. Sweetheart, thank you for introducing me to the magical world of fantasy, which has broadened my creativity. Thank you for making me laugh. Thank you for wiping tears from my face and always seeing the "beautiful and wonderful woman" in me. Thank you for creating a safe space so I can feel loved, supported, encouraged, and wanted. Thank you for continuing to believe in me, even when I didn't see the light at the end of the tunnel. I love you all the way to Pluto and back!

Find out more about Authentic Wellbeing here:

www.authenticwellbeing.net
https://www.instagram.com/authenticwellbeing/
https://www.facebook.com/iskra22
https://www.youtube.com/user/izabela4000
http://unlimitedyou.me

RESOURCES

The Grounding Meditation "You Belong":
   https://mailchi.mp/67db2506b271/youbelong

The Heart-Connecting Meditation:
   https://mailchi.mp/38b92e82a19b/heart

The Morning Prayer to Rejoice in Your Day:
   https://mailchi.mp/9040a108718b/morning_prayer

The Anxiety-Calming Meditation:
   https://mailchi.mp/75fa222f2100/anxiety-calming

Authentic Wellbeing website: www.authenticwellbeing.net

"Make A Wish" Affirmation Card Deck:
   https://mailchi.mp/8e6018eb3456/makeawish

Heart & Body Practices Facebook Community (English
   version):
   https://www.facebook.com/groups/heartbodypractices/

Heart & Body Practices Facebook Community (Polish
   version):
   https://www.facebook.com/groups/praktykisercaiciala/

SUPPORT ME: https://www.paypal.me/izabelachrobak

ABOUT THE AUTHOR

Izabela Chrobak-Tysver, PhD

Izabela Chrobak-Tysver graduated in Poland and Germany as a cardiorespiratory scientist. However, along the way she fell madly in love with practices around self-love, self-acceptance and self-respect. Today, Izabela is a self-worth & true identity ambassador, (w)holistic wellbeing practitioner, teacher, artist and women's life coach who provides guidance to others through programs, blogging, videos and coaching. She is intuitive, an empath, creator, and healer.

She works with women as a wellness and holistic expert, helping them focus on redefining authentic wellbeing on all levels, physical, mental, emotional and spiritual whilst supporting them as they tap into their own inner voices. She believes that the body is the wisest teacher of all times, the most powerful healer you could ever meet and the only mentor you could ever learn the most from.

As a *MAT (Metaphysical Anatomy Technique™)* and *Tetha Healing Practitioner*, Izabela is facilitating virtual and local one-on-one trauma-release healing sessions.

She is the author of the *MAKE A WISH Dandelion Spirit Oracle*

Deck. She is a creator and a host of powerful healing modality called *Heart & Body Practices.*

Currently residing in Wyoming, USA, she runs local workshops and retreats for women, as well as virtual coaching programs.

For more of her work, you can check her out on Instagram **@authenticwellbeing**. Visit also her website www.authenticwellbeing.net, blog https://unlimitedyou.me/, YouTube Channel https://www.youtube.com/user/izabela4000/ and Facebook https://www.facebook.com/iskra22. Join her Heart & Body Practices private Facebook community https://www.facebook.com/groups/heartbodypractices/.

www.ingramcontent.com/pod-product-compliance
Lightning Source LLC
Chambersburg PA
CBHW020150090426
42734CB00008B/770